MORE
IT HAPPENED IN
HOCKEY

Also by Brian McFarlane

IT HAPPENED IN BASEBALL

STANLEY CUP FEVER

IT HAPPENED IN HOCKEY

100 YEARS OF HOCKEY

SITTLER AT CENTER

EVERYTHING YOU WANTED TO KNOW
ABOUT HOCKEY

HOCKEY QUIZ

MORE IT HAPPENED IN HOCKEY

MORE WEIRD & WONDERFUL STORIES FROM CANADA'S GREATEST GAME

BRIAN McFARLANE

Stoddart

Copyright © 1993 by Brian McFarlane

First published in 1993 by
Stoddart Publishing Co. Limited
34 Lesmill Road
Toronto, Canada
M3B 2T6
(416) 445-3333

Canadian Cataloguing in Publication Data

McFarlane, Brian–
More It Happened in Hockey

ISBN 0-7737-5591-8

1. Hockey — Canada.   I. Title

GV848.4.C2M34 1993   796.962'0971   C93-094128-4

Cover Design: Leslie Styles
Cover Photograph: Dan Paul
Design: Brant Cowie/ArtPlus Limited
Typesetting: Tony Gordon Limited
Printed and bound in Canada

Stoddart Publishing gratefully acknowledges the support of the Canada Council, Ontario Ministry of Culture, Tourism, and Recreation, Ontario Arts Council, and Ontario Publishing Centre in the development of writing and publishing in Canada.

*To my grandson
Kelly, age three,
who already
displays a love
for the game*

CONTENTS

PART 1 — Gladiators of the Ice

PART 2 — Bizarre Business

PART 3 — Autocrats and Avatars of the Arena

PART 4 — Lore and Legends

PART

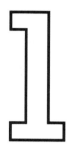

GLADIATORS OF THE ICE

Three Stars for the Rocket

IN THE SPRING of 1944 Maurice "Rocket" Richard of the Montreal Canadiens put on one of the greatest offensive displays in Stanley Cup history. The Canadiens played the Toronto Maple Leafs in a semifinal series that year and Richard, a second-year man who had scored 32 goals during the regular season, was being closely shadowed by big Bob Davidson, a tenacious checker.

After his Canadiens lost by a 3–1 score in the opener, Richard predicted a different outcome in game two. After all, his team had captured the regular season championship, finishing 33 points ahead of the third-place Leafs. But the Leafs kept Richard and the Habs off the score sheet in the first period of game two, and Montreal fans were concerned. Would their favorites ever break out and score a few goals?

Richard relieved their anxiety early in the second period. Two minutes into the period he raced in to beat Paul Bibeault for the game's first goal. Seventeen seconds later he returned and scored again. Toronto fought back with a goal midway through the period, but before the buzzer sounded, Richard took a pass from Toe Blake and scored once more. It was his third goal of the period — a Stanley Cup hat trick.

By then Montreal coach Dick Irvin was shifting Richard from line to line, which confused the Leafs and enabled the Rocket to escape the persistent checking of Davidson. In the third period Richard stayed hot. He scored his fourth goal early in the frame and added a fifth at 8:34. Final score: Richard 5, Toronto 1. The last time a player had scored five

3

or more goals in a playoff game was back in 1917 when Bernie Morris of Seattle scored six against the Canadiens.

There is now, and was then, a popular tradition of selecting three stars after each NHL game, with the third star being introduced first. Fans at the Forum that night roared with anger when the public address announcer intoned, "Tonight's third star — Rocket Richard!" How could that be? How could the Rocket score all five goals and be a lowly third star?

The announcer continued over the howling of the fans. "Star number two — Rocket Richard!"

Now the fans began to catch on. Cheers and applause erupted throughout the Forum, and fans threw hats and programs into the air even before the announcer made his dramatic third announcement. "And tonight's first star — Maurice 'Rocket' Richard!"

The fans treated Richard to one of the greatest ovations ever. It was the only time an NHL player was awarded all three stars.

Did Cyclone Score While Skating Backward?

FOR DECADES AFTER HE STARRED for the Renfrew Creamery Kings in the 1910–11 season, Cyclone Taylor refused to confirm that he once scored a goal while skating backward. But he didn't deny it, either. When I asked him about it — he was in his nineties then — he chuckled and said, "Why don't you ask someone who was at the game?" Well, it was somewhat difficult to locate a living survivor among the 3,000 or so fans who

4

attended that long-ago game in Renfrew, but newspaper accounts of the contest appear to confirm that such a goal was scored.

That season a bitter rivalry existed between Ottawa and Renfrew, and Taylor, in conversation with his friend Ottawa goalie Percy Lesueur one day, stated that it might be "no trouble at all to take a pass in full flight, spin around, and score a goal against Ottawa while skating backward." Taylor said later that he was only joking, but when his comment was printed in an Ottawa newspaper, the Capital City fans were furious. The next time he appeared for Renfrew on Ottawa ice they hurled bottles and rotten fruit at him.

He was unable to score in that game, but in a return match in Renfrew a few nights later, and with an arena full of fans urging him on, he made good his boast by spinning around in front of Lesueur, skating backward for several feet, and scoring with a hard shot to the upper corner.

But Taylor's unique goal wasn't the only reason that game became a memorable one. Renfrew owner M. J. O'Brien, a multimillionaire, offered a team bonus of $100 for each goal scored in the game and a personal reward of $50 to every player who scored one. Spurred on by the owner's promise, Renfrew walloped Ottawa 17–2, and O'Brien cheerfully doled out $2,250 in bonus money, a fortune in that era.

The Green–Maki Incident

OR SOME UNKNOWN REASON the 1969–70 preseason NHL exhibition games were rampant with brawls. The most serious flare-up

5

occurred on September 21 in Ottawa in a game between the Boston Bruins and the St. Louis Blues.

Derek Sanderson of the Bruins recalls talking to teammate Ted Green before the game and hearing him say, "You won't see me hitting anyone out there tonight. I'm still negotiating a new contract. When I'm signed, then I'll hit."

Sanderson, sidelined with a sore knee, watched from the stands as Wayne Maki, a swift but unspectacular winger with the Blues, moved around Green during the game. They bumped and suddenly Maki swung at Green with his stick. Green retaliated by throwing a punch at Maki, knocking him down. Maki jumped up and speared Green. Then Green slashed Maki on the arm, and for a split second that appeared to be the end of it. But as Green turned to skate away, headed for the penalty box, Maki hit the Bruin squarely over the head with his stick. Green collapsed and lay on the ice, unconscious and bleeding.

Bobby Orr leaped off the bench and smacked Maki. Then Ace Bailey belted him. But the sight of Green lying on the ice knocked the toughness out of all the players. The right side of Green's head was crushed and his left side was partially paralyzed. His speech was slurred. Sanderson recalls saying to himself, "Here's the toughest guy on skates and he's in big, big trouble."

Green was rushed to an Ottawa hospital and underwent a five-hour brain operation. A few days later other surgery followed, including the insertion of a metal plate in his skull.

The suspensions handed out seem ludicrous in retrospect. At the time they were called "the stiffest in league annals." Maki was suspended for 30 days and Green for 13 games if and when he returned to

6

action. It was assumed he never would. Police laid charges against both players, the first of their kind in NHL history.

Weeks later both men were exonerated after testifying in an Ottawa courtroom. A year later Green made what was called "a miraculous comeback" and played effectively for the Bruins. The following year he was a key performer on Boston's 1970 Stanley Cup–winning team. After that he played a few years in the WHA and retired following the 1978–79 season. When he left the game, he spoke out against violence in hockey and asked owners to put an end to it.

Ironically Maki's NHL career was cut short by a brain tumor, discovered while he was playing for the Vancouver Canucks in 1972. He died in the spring of 1974.

Even though the Green injury shocked most NHL players, they still weren't prepared to adopt helmets as protection against similar incidents. The Bruins tried to force helmets on their players, issuing headgear to Bobby Orr and others. When coach Milt Schmidt saw his players at practice one day without their helmets, he ordered them to put them on or get off the ice. Orr looked at him, then slowly skated off the ice, followed by the rest of the Bruins. Schmidt decided not to make an issue of it and the helmets were stored away.

Ken Dryden's Remarkable Debut

THE KID HAD BEEN A STAR in college hockey at Cornell. He had played well with the Montreal farm team in Halifax. He was tall, wore

7

glasses, and was said to be very bright, an intellectual. That was about all we knew about rookie netminder Ken Dryden back in 1971 when he was called up to the Canadiens. That and the fact his brother Dave was also a goalie.

It was late in the season and the Habs were on their way to a third-place finish when they gave Dryden a half-dozen starts in goal. He surprised everybody by winning every game.

When the Canadiens opened the playoffs against Boston, they were said to be in too deep. The Bruins had smashed a handful of records on their way to a first-place finish. They had Bobby Orr, Phil Esposito, Wayne Cashman, Ken Hodge, and Johnny Bucyk, plus home ice advantage in the series.

The Bruins were pleased to see Dryden start in goal for Montreal. They'd soon show him what

Ken Dryden stood tall in the Montreal Canadiens' net during the battling seventies. (Robert B. Shaver)

8

playoff pressure was all about. As expected, Boston took the opener 3–1, while in game two the Bruins raced out to a 5–1 lead.

Suddenly the Canadiens found a groove and fought back. They scored a goal, then another, then four more to take a 7–5 lead. The Bruins were rattled by the second-period barrage, but they weren't about to concede. They regrouped for a third-period attack on Dryden.

But the lanky goaltender turned aside shot after shot. Some of his saves were truly magnificent. And when the final buzzer sounded, he almost fainted from the constant pressure he had been under.

His confidence bolstered by the comeback in game two, Dryden continued to give Montreal spectacular goaltending, and the Canadiens eventually eliminated the frustrated Bruins in seven games. Phil Esposito, who had scored a record 76 goals during the regular season, couldn't believe "the big giraffe" in the Montreal net had held him to just three goals in the series.

The Canadiens went on to eliminate the Chicago Blackhawks in the final series, with Dryden again playing a key role in the victory. At season's end he was awarded the Conn Smythe Trophy as MVP of the playoffs, a remarkable achievement for an inexperienced newcomer with only six regular season games under his big pads.

The following season he continued to play brilliantly and skated off with the Calder Trophy as the league's top freshman. No player in history had been a playoff MVP one season and a rookie award winner the next. It happened to Dryden. It may never happen again.

The Legendary Frank McGee

AT THE TURN OF THE CENTURY a young Ottawa forward named Frank McGee established himself as one of the finest hockey players in the world. To many fans of the era he was the greatest stickhandler who ever carried a puck down the ice.

Young McGee began playing hockey against his family's wishes. He started his career as a student at the University of Ottawa, and before long he was the star of the fabled Ottawa Silver Seven, Stanley Cup champions.

One night, early in his career, McGee's team tangled with the rowdy Montreal Wanderers. Toughest of the Wanderers was the hard-rock Pokey Leahy, and before the game was a few minutes old Leahy caught McGee by surprise and smashed into him, sending him crashing to the ice. McGee was carried off, bleeding from a head wound, and later, as a result of that check, he lost the sight in his left eye.

McGee recovered in time, and despite the urging of his friends and parents to give up the game, he returned to hockey. Just as fast and as dangerous with the puck as ever, he seldom talked about his accident, although he did threaten to catch up to Pokey Leahy one day and pay him back for the check that almost ended his career.

In the following years McGee set some amazing records. During one Stanley Cup game against Dawson City, he scored 14 goals, a mark no player has ever tied or topped. He once scored four goals in one minute and four seconds. In 1905, wearing tape

10

to protect a broken wrist, he scored the tying and winning goals for Ottawa in a Stanley Cup–clinching game. That night McGee wore tape around both wrists to confuse opposing players who would certainly have slashed him on the broken one.

Then came the night when Frank McGee's path again crossed that of Pokey Leahy. When the teams lined up for the opening face-off, McGee told Leahy he was out to settle an old score. Leahy snarled back, "You try it, Frankie, and I'll knock your other eye out."

But McGee was determined to try it. He came roaring down the ice and crashed into Leahy. They both went down, but Leahy was unable to get up. He was badly hurt and had to be carried off on a stretcher. Never again did he lace on skates to play hockey.

The collision with Leahy was one of the few times McGee deliberately tried to hurt another player. Normally he was a clean player who was idolized for his stylish play and good looks. His hockey pants were always freshly laundered and creased with an iron. An immaculately groomed man, McGee never failed to comb his blond hair neatly to one side.

He was a born leader, and when the First World War broke out, he was able to serve in the infantry despite the loss of his eye. To get around the handicap, he simply had a friend enlist in his name. Once in the army, he quickly rose from private to captain. In the winter of 1916, though, during one of the war's fiercest battles in France, an enemy shell ended the life of Frank McGee, one of hockey's greatest heroes.

11

A Scorer's Mistake Cost Bobby Hull the Record

IN THE SPRING OF 1962 Chicago's Bobby Hull was in hot pursuit of a goal-scoring record shared by two Montreal Canadiens — Rocket Richard and Boom Boom Geoffrion. They were the only two players ever to score 50 goals in 50 games. Hull had a remarkable second half in 1962. He scored 35 goals in 31 games, which allowed him to tie Richard and Geoffrion's formidable record.

The Golden Jet's second-half surge also vaulted him into a tie with the Rangers' Andy Bathgate for the individual scoring title and the Art Ross Trophy. Both men finished with 84 points, but it was Hull who captured the Ross award because of his greater number of goals (50 to 28).

All but forgotten was a goal Hull scored early in the season, a goal that would have given him a record-breaking 51 in 50 games and would have made him a clear-cut winner of the scoring crown. In a game against Detroit a few weeks into the season, Hull blasted a shot at Red Wing goalie Terry Sawchuk. His shot was deflected by a stick in front of Sawchuk's crease, and the official scorer awarded the goal to Hull's linemate Ab McDonald.

After the game, McDonald told the referee he hadn't touched the puck. He claimed that it had gone in off the stick of a Red Wing defenseman and that Hull should have received credit for the goal. But McDonald had waited too long to point out the mistake. The official report of the game had already been filed with the league office and nothing could be done to change the verdict. The mistake didn't

12

bother Hull at the time. He just shrugged it off. On the final day of the season, however, someone reminded him that the goal given to McDonald had cost him the 51-goal record.

Gretzky Catches Howe

IT WAS ONLY FITTING that it happened in Edmonton. On October 15, 1989, the former hometown hero, Wayne Gretzky, returned to smash one of hockey's longest-standing individual records — Gordie Howe's mark of 1,850 career points.

And he did it in typical Gretzky style, scoring a goal in the last minute of regulation time to tie the score 4–4. The goal was the Great One's 1,851st point, and it stopped the game for several minutes. Gordie Howe, who said he was "cheering like hell when the goal went in," came out of the stands to congratulate Wayne and present him with a gift. League president John Ziegler and Mark Messier, the Oiler captain and Gretzky's best friend, added their congratulations. Messier presented Gretzky with a bracelet fitted with 1.851 carats of diamonds spelling out "1,851."

The record-setting goal was produced by a short backhand shot, a technique Howe had told Gretzky years earlier to work on. Gretzky pumped the puck behind Bill Ranford for his 1,851st point in his 780th NHL game. It had taken Howe 26 years and 1,767 games with Detroit and Hartford to set the standard the Great One so easily eclipsed.

"Gordie is still the greatest in my mind and in the minds of everyone else," Gretzky said. "Remember, his points were scored in a different era. The game

13

was a lot different then. Players just weren't scoring 100 points per season."

"I don't know how he does these things so dramatically," Howe said of Gretzky's accomplishment. "There's no sense of loss. I held the record for a long time [almost 30 years] and I hope to be around when he scores 3,000 points."

Gretzky took a hammering in the game and was lucky to be around at the finish. After assisting on Bernie Nicholls' first-period goal, earning the point that tied the record, he took a hit from John Beukaboom in the second and was in a daze for several minutes.

"He was very dizzy and I had to keep checking on him," Kings coach Tom Webster said. "But by the third period he was back to normal. He had his old jump back."

Indeed he did, enough to smash the record with time running out. And enough to add to his total and win the game 5–4 with a whirl-around-the-net move that saw him beat Ranford again at 3:24 into overtime.

When the Hockey Hall of Fame requested the helmet, gloves, and stick used in the historic game, Gretzky quickly obliged. He said another 13 sticks used in the game would go to his dad, Walter Gretzky, who would pass them along to various charities for fund-raising purposes.

The Fight John Ferguson Waited For

WHEN JOHN FERGUSON was 14 years old, he was the envy of his hockey-playing pals. The teenager already had a position

14

in professional hockey: he was the official stickboy for the Vancouver Canucks of the Western Hockey League.

Years later, when he was helping the Montreal Canadiens win Stanley Cups, when he was known as the NHL's most feared enforcer, fans wondered what motivated him to play the way he did. Why did he fiercely protect his teammates? Why was he willing to slug it out with the toughest players in the game?

Perhaps the pattern of his aggressive and some-times violent approach to hockey was established one night in Vancouver, while he was filling water bottles and tending the team sticks during a game between Vancouver and the Edmonton Eskimos. At the time, one of John's idols on the Canucks was soft-spoken Phil Maloney, the WHL's leading scorer. During the game, there was a skirmish in front of the Canuck bench and Maloney was attacked by Larry Zeidel, a hard-nosed Eskimo defenseman. Right in front of the horrified stickboy, Zeidel dropped his gloves and clubbed Maloney with rights and lefts. When Maloney fell to the ice, Zeidel fell on him and administered a pummeling that left Maloney dazed and bleeding.

Then Zeidel stood and challenged the rest of the players on the Vancouver bench to do something about it. Nobody did. But Ferguson, the teenage stickboy, was left seething with rage. He was furious with Zeidel for beating up on his idol and furious with the Canucks for not coming off the bench to help a teammate in trouble. If Ferguson had been a little older and a little bigger, he would have leaped at the throat of the burly defenseman, no matter how foolish it might have been.

15

Ten years went by and Ferguson, now 24 years old, had found his own place in the game. He was a well-respected winger with Cleveland of the American Hockey League. In a game with Hershey one night he came face-to-face with veteran Larry Zeidel, the toughest player in the circuit.

"Suddenly that fight in Vancouver a decade earlier flashed through my mind," Ferguson would say later. "I could see poor Maloney sagging to the ice and Zeidel pounding him. I'm sure Zeidel had forgotten it, but I never would. Then I got the perfect opportunity to do something about it. Zeidel whacked me with his stick up around my head."

When Zeidel clubbed the Cleveland rookie, Fergie whirled, threw off his gloves, and slammed into Zeidel, who was taken by surprise. He didn't know Ferguson from a goalpost and had no idea the kid was seeking revenge for the Maloney beating long ago.

The bout was brief and brutal. Ferguson's big fists slammed into Zeidel's face and head. The veteran's knees buckled and he staggered. Another solid blow to the face knocked him out.

When the officials pulled Ferguson toward the penalty box, he snarled back at the unconscious Zeidel, "That's for Phil Maloney!"

It's Raining Rubber

WHEN THE QUEBEC NORDIQUES faced the Boston Bruins at the Boston Garden on March 21, 1991, Quebec goalie Ron Tugnutt knew he was in for a busy evening. He would be facing renowned shooters like Cam Neely

16

and Ray Bourque and he expected a heavy work load. But he didn't expect to be worn to a frazzle.

The 155-pound Tugnutt was pelted at the rate of more than a shot every minute, most of them sizzlers. But time and again the nimble netminder denied the Bruins of glorious opportunities. With the game knotted at 3–3, Tugnutt put on a display of overtime goaltending that brought the Bruin faithful to their feet in a seldom seen tribute to a gallant opponent.

With seconds left to play in the overtime frame, Tugnutt robbed both Bourque and Neely of near-certain goals to salvage a tie and a single point for his team. When the final buzzer sounded, the young man had stopped 70 of 73 shots to earn the respect and admiration of everyone in the building.

As the crowd stood and roared, Cam Neely skated up to the exhausted Tugnutt and said, "Take a bow. It's you they're applauding."

Most of the fans assumed the 73 shots on Tugnutt set a league record. Not so. The mark for most shots in a game is held by a former Chicago netminder, Sam Lopresti, who was bombarded by 83 Boston shots in a game played at the Garden 50 years earlier, almost to the day. Incredibly Lopresti almost stole a win for the Hawks that night, finally losing 3–2.

The patriotic Lopresti joined the U.S. Navy shortly afterward, saying, "It may be safer facing Nazi U-boats in the Atlantic than dodging hockey pucks in the NHL." Ironically he had plenty of time to consider that sentiment when his ship was torpedoed and he managed to survive for 45 days adrift on a life raft.

Eddie Shore's Hazardous Journey

WHEN EDDIE SHORE, the Edmonton Express, moved from the Pacific Coast League to the NHL in 1926 he became an instant superstar with the Boston Bruins, a tough, fearless, indestructible defenseman who would win MVP honors four times. Art Ross, Boston's general manager, often held Shore back from the player introductions prior to a game. Then he would have the band play "Hail to the Chief" while Shore made a grand entrance wearing a gold dressing gown over his uniform. When Shore nodded that he was ready to play, a valet would remove the gown.

One day Shore missed the train carrying the Bruins from Boston to Montreal. He phoned a friend, a wealthy Boston fan, and borrowed the man's big limousine and his chauffeur. Then he took off in pursuit of his teammates.

EDDIE SHORE

Eddie Shore, the Edmonton Express, has some fun with the puck.
(Hockey Hall of Fame)

18

When Shore reached the Green Mountains of Vermont, he found himself in the middle of a blizzard. The terrified chauffeur, after spinning his wheels on the slippery mountain roads, wanted to turn back. Shore pushed the man out of the driver's seat and took the wheel himself. He could barely see the highway, and four or five times he found himself sliding into the ditch. On one occasion he sought the help of a farmer who hitched up a team of horses to haul the limo out of a snowdrift.

Driving all night and all the next day, Shore arrived at the Montreal Forum just before game time. His hands were raw and frostbitten, and he looked so haggard and exhausted that his coach suggested he see a doctor and then go straight to his hotel room for a good night's sleep.

Shore refused and grabbed his skates and hockey gear. He played the full sixty minutes against the fast-moving Montreal Maroons and turned in a flawless defensive performance. He even made a few dashes into the offensive zone. In fact, on one of these forays he slammed in the game's only goal, which made the long, hazardous journey through the mountains worth the effort.

Berenson's Six Goals Still a Record

HE WAS A GOOD-LOOKING redheaded centerman, a Michigan graduate who wanted to play pro hockey. Nobody thought he would, not at the NHL level. No American college grad had ever jumped to the NHL. Why should Red Berenson be any different?

19

But he was different. He was a shade faster and a bit smarter with the puck than his college confreres. And he did crack the lineup of the Montreal Canadiens in 1961. He stayed around to play on a Montreal Stanley Cup–winning team in 1965, one of the big thrills of his NHL career.

Berenson moved on to play with the Rangers and the Blues, and it was after he donned a St. Louis uniform that he blossomed into one of the top scorers in hockey. One unforgettable game took place on November 7, 1968. It was a road game against the Philadelphia Flyers, and Berenson was in the middle of a slump. The season was a month old and he had scored just one goal.

But there was magic in his hands and stick that night against goalie Doug Favell and the Flyers. Every time Berenson touched the puck the red light flashed behind Favell. The redheaded centerman scored six goals in the game, a record for a road game, as the Blues shut out the Flyers 8–0.

"The odd thing is, I might have scored two or three more in the game," Berenson said later. "I hit one goalpost and missed on a couple of other good chances. It was a great confidence booster after my dismal start that year. And what really amazes me is that neither Lemieux nor Gretzky have tied or beaten my mark. I never thought it would stand for 25 years."

Berenson was presented with a new station wagon by the Blues' owners in recognition of his feat. When he sold the vehicle to broadcaster Dan Kelly a few days later, he angered team management, and it wasn't long before he was traded to Detroit as part of a deal for Garry Unger. In a career that spanned 17 NHL seasons, Red scored 261 goals.

20

Does Anybody Remember Warren Young?

FROM 1980 THROUGH 1984 Warren Young's hockey career amounted to little more than a depressing bus ride through minor league cities such as Nashville, Oklahoma City, Birmingham, and Baltimore. He was thankful he had graduated from college (Michigan Tech) because his minor league stats hadn't attracted much interest from NHL clubs.

When he was invited to Pittsburgh's training camp prior to the 1984–85 season, he knew it was his last chance to make an impression. He was in his 29th year, a doddering old man by hockey standards.

For some reason, rookie sensation Mario Lemieux, then 19, liked Young's style and asked to be placed on the same line. Despite the ten-year age difference, the two fitted together like hand and glove. Young had never seen the kind of passes Mario deftly placed on his stick. He converted a large number of them into goals and finished the season with 40 lamplighters (only three fewer than Lemieux) and had 32 assists plus a berth on the rookie All-Star squad.

"They were a magic act," Jim Christie wrote in Toronto's *Globe and Mail,* "but it was Mario who was the magician."

He was indeed. Despite being called "the laziest player in the NHL" by TV commentator Don Cherry, Lemieux helped convert Young from an unknown minor leaguer into a much-publicized big league celebrity. His teammates praised Young's accomplishments and kidded him about his late arrival, calling him Warren Old and Geritol. They decided not to initiate him with the traditional head shave when one of them pointed out, "At his age it may never grow back."

Good fortune smiled on Young again the following season. It was the year Detroit went on a spending spree, signing a number of free agents to million-dollar deals. Young was one of them. He signed a multiyear contract with the Wings that had him earning twice as much as Lemieux's base salary of $125,000.

But without Lemieux to set him up, Young found that goals were harder to score in Detroit. He would never again recapture the glory that was his in Pittsburgh. He would forever be known as the player who rode Mario's passes to a single unforgettable season. After a couple of mediocre years in a Red Wing uniform, Young faded from the scene.

A Big Star, but Not an All-Star

GOALIE AL ROLLINS HAD a terrific season for the Chicago Blackhawks in 1954, and even though his team finished dead last in the standings, at season's end Rollins was awarded the Hart Trophy as the NHL's most valuable player. Amazingly Rollins was overlooked by the All-Star selectors that season. They placed Toronto's Harry Lumley on the first team and Terry Sawchuk on the second, which raises the question, how can a player be voted best in the league and not be an All-Star? But Rollins was accustomed to being snubbed by hockey's award voters. In 1951 he cap-

22

tured the Vezina Trophy as top NHL goaltender. He was passed over in the All-Star balloting that season, too. Detroit's Sawchuk was voted number one and Chuck Rayner of New York was the second-team choice.

The Bizarre Tragedy of Spinner Spencer

THOSE OF US WHO have been associated with *Hockey Night in Canada* for a quarter century or more will never forget a Saturday night telecast during the 1969–70 season. Toronto Maple Leaf rookie Brian "Spinner" Spencer, an exciting addition to the Leaf roster, a kid with wavy blond hair, choirboy looks, and an irresistible personality, was to be host Ward Cornell's guest during the intermission of the Toronto game with Chicago.

While we looked forward to seeing Spencer's television debut, there was much greater anticipation of the event in far-off Fort St. James, British Columbia, Spencer's hometown. Brian's father, Roy Spencer, was bursting with pride that night. Not only had Brian's wife given birth to a baby girl two days earlier, but his son had made it all the way from the backyard rink to the mammoth ice surfaces of the NHL, and now millions of fans would get to see him — up close and personal, as they say.

But Roy Spencer was suddenly denied the opportunity to see his boy trade quips with Ward Cornell. He listened in disbelief as a CBC announcer informed him that the network affiliate in Prince George was switching from the Toronto–Chicago game to the Vancouver Canucks–Oakland Seals

23

contest. Roy Spencer roared with frustration and outrage. How could the CBC do this do him?

He grabbed a rifle, stormed out of the house, and jumped into his truck. At high speed he drove the 90 miles to the CBC station in Prince George and skidded to a halt in the parking lot. Barging into the station and waving his rifle, he ordered the staff to line up against the wall. He demanded that one of them switch the channel to the Toronto game. When told by terrified staffers that it couldn't be done, Spencer ran back to the parking lot where, brandishing his rifle at approaching police officers, he met a tragic end. He was felled by three RCMP bullets fired from close range. Spencer dropped dead in his tracks. Meanwhile, in many parts of Canada, a million hockey fans were absorbed in his son's conversation with Ward Cornell.

Hockey bad boy Brian Spencer as a Buffalo Sabre.
(Robert B. Shaver)

24

From that point on, trouble seemed to stalk Brian Spencer relentlessly. Colorful, tough, and fearless, he had a tremendous physique. He played for four NHL clubs — the Leafs, Sabres, Islanders, and Penguins — but scored only 80 goals in 10 NHL seasons, hardly the stats of the star he wanted to be.

Martin O'Malley, who detailed his life story in *Gross Misconduct: The Life of Spinner Spencer,* once said of him, "To me he personified Canadian hockey in ways that Orr and Gretzky never did. He showed what you can do with sheer hard work and never-quit perseverance. And he loved the press . . . loved to tell stories."

In time, long after he hung up his skates, Brian Spencer became the story. And it wasn't a pretty one.

He was arrested by Florida police in 1987 and taken in handcuffs from a rundown trailer in a backwater swamp where he lived with a hooker. The charge was murder. He was accused, five years after the fact, of shooting to death Michael Dalfo, a man who had abused the prostitute who shared Spencer's trailer.

Evidence was provided by Spencer's former girlfriend Diane Fialco, who said she went to Dalfo's house on February 2, 1982, as a "professional escort." She left when Dalfo appeared to be high on cocaine, she testified. Later that night she and Spencer returned to the Dalfo house. Spencer forced Dalfo into their car, took him to a deserted area, and allegedly shot him to death.

But the prosecution had difficulty building a strong case against Spencer. In less than an hour, on October 16, a Palm Beach jury found him not guilty of first-degree murder. Had the seven-man, five-woman jury found him guilty, he would have faced a possible 25-year prison term without parole — or even death in the electric chair.

25

But tragedy, like a persistent checker in hockey, kept hounding Spencer. Despite the urging of friends to leave Florida, the former hockey player said he "didn't like the cold and couldn't afford the housing."

On the night of June 2, 1988, he told a new lady friend, Monica Jarboe, "See you in half an hour." He left their apartment and never returned. A few minutes later he was gunned down, the victim of an unknown killer.

Spencer was murdered while driving with his friend Greg Cook through a dangerous section of Riviera Beach, Florida. Cook, after stopping to buy $10 worth of crack cocaine, stopped again farther down the road for cigarettes. While he was looking for his money, an armed assailant approached the car and put a gun to Cook's head. Cook produced a few bills, but Spencer told the gunman he had no money. The mugger shot Spencer, and the bullet traveled through his arm and crashed into his chest. He died almost instantly.

It was not a contract killing, as many at first believed, but simply a case of Spencer being in the wrong place at the wrong time. Months later a man with a criminal record was arrested and confessed to Spencer's murder. He was subsequently sentenced to life in prison.

William Bops Bowman

IT WAS A BLOW to the head that nobody saw, but there was enough circumstantial evidence to indict NHL tough guy Tiger Williams of the Vancouver Canucks.

It happened in the third game of a 1980 playoff series between the Buffalo Sabres, then coached by Scotty Bowman, and the Vancouver Canucks. At the time Bowman was en route to becoming the NHL's winningest mentor, and Williams was carving a path to the title "hockey's all-time bad man." Eventually he finished with a record 3,966 penalty minutes.

Williams was at his nastiest in game three of the series after his Canucks fell behind two games to none. At one stage of the game played in Vancouver he chopped Sabre forward Bobby Mongrain with his stick, prompting screams from Bowman and the Buffalo players on the bench.

The gritty Mongrain shook off the blow and carried the puck into the Vancouver zone, where he was smashed into the boards by a Vancouver defenseman. Mongrain was injured on the play and lay motionless on the ice.

All eyes were on the diminutive Sabre. They must have been, because apparently nobody witnessed what happened next over at the Buffalo bench. Suddenly coach Bowman went sprawling backward and was knocked cold. He wound up flat on his back at the feet of his astonished players.

When he was revived, the groggy Bowman complained that Williams had hammered him over the head with his hockey stick while all eyes were on Mongrain. "It was a real two-hander," Bowman beefed. "He whacked me and nobody saw it."

After the game, when questioned about Bowman's accusation, Williams gave reporters an innocent look and said he didn't remember any incident involving Bowman during the game. Later he told me that Bowman had a bad habit of leaning

27

out over the boards during the play. "When a coach does that, Brian," he said, "sometimes accidents will happen."

What Williams didn't know — nor do most people — is that Bowman has a plate in his head, the aftermath of a serious hockey injury suffered during his junior playing days. A stick creasing his head could have killed him.

Prior to game four in the series, Brian O'Neill, executive vice president of the NHL, announced that Williams would have to serve a one-game suspension. O'Neill claimed he had seen enough videotape evidence to reach that verdict. Williams didn't play, the Sabres won the series, and the Canucks' season was over. To this day Williams hasn't confessed to the crime. "Gee, I don't remember hitting Bowman," he says with just the hint of a grin.

Wherever Tiger Williams went, trouble was sure to follow. (John Maiola)

28

Unbelievable! A Defenseman Wins the Scoring Crown

IN THE LATE SIXTIES and early seventies Boston's Bobby Orr was the most electrifying player in hockey. Before Orr came along hockey people thought it was impossible for a defenseman to win the individual scoring title in the NHL.

Orr changed their thinking in a hurry. In 1969–70 he amazed everyone by finishing on top of the scoring race with 120 points, 21 more than teammate Phil Esposito. No defenseman had ever come close to winning a scoring title. It was unthinkable.

To prove it was no fluke Orr finished on top again five years later, this time with 135 points. In between he finished second three times and third once (all four times behind Esposito). What made his accomplishments even more remarkable was that he played for most of his career on aching knees that required numerous operations.

And while Orr's scoring titles have been well publicized, one of his most amazing marks hasn't been — his career plus-minus rating. For his 657-game career Bobby was a plus 597. That means he was on the ice for 1,188 even-strength goals and on for only 591 goals against.

Tom Reid's First Shift

TOM REID, A DEFENSEMAN with Chicago and Minnesota for 11 NHL seasons, vividly recalls his first game in the NHL. "I remember the game clearly, but my first shift in the game is a little fuzzy in my mind," he says. "I was brought up to Chicago, and

29

coach Billy Reay sent me on the ice early in the game. We were playing against the Red Wings and Gordie Howe. Big Gordie was Detroit's star player at the time, and I made a mental note to beware of him.

"I'd been on the ice for a few seconds when the puck came to me and I cleared it out of our zone. That's when I was hit as hard as I'd ever been hit in my life. I don't know where he came from, but Gordie nailed me to the fence. I was knocked out for a few seconds, and when I opened my eyes and tried to get up, I fell down again. My knees were rubbery and my vision was blurred. My eyes were watering, and when I wobbled over to our bench, I began to panic because I couldn't see out of my right eye. I remember being near tears, thinking I'd been blinded and had my brains scrambled on my very first shift at the tender age of 19.

"When I reached the bench, coach Reay looked surprised. 'Reid, what the hell are you doing back here so soon?' he roared.

"'Coach,' I said, 'that old man with Detroit just blinded me. I can't see a thing out of my right eye.'

"Billy laughed and said, 'No wonder.' He grabbed my helmet and twisted it around until it was back on straight. Once he did that I could see again instantly. It was beautiful.

"I didn't think to ask him if he could do anything to fix my splitting headache."

Rags to Riches

IN THE EARLY SEVENTIES Charlie Simmer was just another minor leaguer. Too slow for the NHL, all the experts said, although they liked his size and his attitude. Charlie had played a few games as a checking centerman with the California Seals and a few more with the same club when they became the Cleveland Barons. When he was released by the Barons, he signed a minor league contract with the Los Angeles Kings organization, but his future looked bleak.

"Poor Charlie doesn't have NHL speed" was the verdict of two Kings coaches, Ron Stewart and Bob Berry, "especially for a centerman."

"Why don't you fellows play him at left wing, his natural position?" Kings general manager George McGuire asked.

"I'll keep it in mind," Berry replied. Meanwhile Simmer languished in the minors and rode the buses from city to city. It was a depressing existence, and Charlie decided that if he didn't get a break soon, he'd give up hockey and find a nine-to-five job somewhere.

His break came midway through the 1978–79 season. A series of injuries hit the Kings, and Berry called on Simmer. This time he played him at left wing, with Marcel Dionne at center and Dave Taylor on the right side, forming the Triple Crown Line. For the next few seasons it was the most feared line in hockey.

Simmer's scoring touch delighted Kings fans, and he closed out the season by scoring goals in five straight games. When the 1979–80 season got under way, he potted goals in the first six games. That amounted to a streak of eleven straight goal-scoring games, surpassing a league record of 10, held jointly by Andy Bathgate and Mike Bossy.

But the NHL refused to recognize Simmer's streak because it spanned two seasons. There was only one

31

thing to do — start another streak. In game after game Charlie pumped in goals from far out and in close. He scored on breakaways, rebounds, and tip-ins. And he wasn't stopped until he'd scored 17 goals in 13 consecutive games — a modern-day NHL record.

Despite spending most of the first five years of his career in the minors, Charlie Simmer went on to play 711 NHL games. He recorded back-to-back 56-goal seasons, made the All-Star team, and won the Bill Masterton Trophy for his qualities of perseverance (he had that in abundance), sportsmanship, and dedication to hockey. He even married a *Playboy* playmate of the year. Not a bad career turnaround for a player who "couldn't skate."

Hockey's Iron Man Might Have Been a Leaf

BACK IN 1975 the Montreal Canadiens had a problem. They were searching for a solid defensive forward, preferably a centerman who could win face-offs.

Scotty Bowman, the Habs' coach, was engaged in casual conversation with Roger Neilson one day. Neilson, then coaching the junior Peterborough Petes, happened to mention that one of his players, Doug Jarvis, was the best face-off man in hockey.

"Of course you mean in junior hockey," Bowman said.

"No, I mean in all of hockey," Neilson replied.

With this information stuck firmly in his mind, Bowman went to Sam Pollock, general manager of the Canadiens, and asked, "How can we acquire

32

Jarvis? Roger Neilson tells me he's the best face-off man in hockey."

Pollock admitted Jarvis might be a problem to acquire because he had been drafted earlier that year by the Toronto Maple Leafs. So, one of the first things Pollock did was to make sure Leaf owner Harold Ballard was aware that Jarvis was a devout Christian. He asked Ballard, "How is that religious kid you drafted doing?" Ballard's antipathy toward "religious" players had been firmly established when he dumped Laurie Boschman, another good centerman and born-again Christian.

Then, in trade talks with Leaf general manager Jim Gregory, Pollock mentioned a player named Greg Hubick, a Montreal farmhand. "He needs a chance to play, and we've no room for him. Maybe he could help your Leafs," he told Gregory.

Gregory said he could use Hubick, but asked, "Who can I give up in return?"

"Why not make out a list of five players in your farm system and I'll pick one in return for Hubick," Pollock suggested.

Gregory's list included a couple of players he thought Pollock would find too attractive to pass up. He must have been surprised when Pollock selected the fifth name on the list — Doug Jarvis.

At the Montreal training camp there was only one spot open on the Hab roster — and rookie Jarvis grabbed it. He excelled at winning face-offs and his defensive play was superb. He played in every game and his team won the Stanley Cup. They won it again in 1977, 1978, and 1979. Jarvis barely missed a shift in four straight seasons and collected four Stanley Cup rings.

He played 80 games in each of seven seasons for

Montreal before he was traded to Washington as part of a blockbuster deal — Jarvis, Rod Langway, Brian Engblom, and Craig Laughlin for Ryan Walter and Rick Green. In Washington he played three more 80-game seasons before moving on to Hartford in another deal. His attendance record at Whaler games was also perfect. On December 26, 1986, he surpassed Gary Unger's consecutive-game record of 914. Jarvis went on to establish the current NHL ironman mark of 962 games, which dates back to April 5, 1987.

He came close to missing a game only once, when he was knocked out during a game in Detroit. Team doctors kept him in hospital overnight, then gave him the green light to play that evening.

And his fondest memory?

"Game number one. Just stepping on the ice at the Montreal Forum that night was the fulfillment of a lifelong dream."

Credit Morenz for Big League Hockey in New York

MENTION THE NAME Howie Morenz to hockey old-timers and the superlatives fall like water over Niagara. King Clancy, who played against him, once said, "Morenz was the greatest I ever saw. He was as fast as a bullet and had a shot to match. He could stop on a dime and give you five cents change. The first time I played against him he sifted right through the Ottawa defense and scored. I said to him, 'Kid, you do that again and I'll cut your legs off.' He said to me, 'Clancy, I'll be right back.' Seconds later, there he was again, cutting right between my partner and me and scoring again. I couldn't believe the little bugger could move that fast."

Morenz was to hockey what Babe Ruth was to baseball. But in New York, North America's sporting capital in the twenties, neither hockey nor its biggest star figured prominently in America's sports future. Promoter Tex Rickard was building Madison Square Garden, but he saw no reason to install machinery for making artificial ice.

Then another entrepreneur, Tom Duggan, a hockey fanatic who had finagled three franchises from the NHL for a mere $7,000, became involved. Duggan knew that a New York franchise was critical for the success of hockey in the U.S., but Rickard had to be sold on the merits of the ice game.

Duggan persuaded Rickard to journey to Montreal with him and see the great Morenz in action. Rickard, accompanied by the famous columnist and sports fan Damon Runyon, made the trip north, and both visitors were thrilled by the play of Morenz and the Canadiens. Rickard returned to Broadway and ordered his architects to make some changes. An ice-making facility must be added to the plans for his new arena.

When the New York Americans, in their star-spangled uniforms, hosted the Montreal Canadiens in their NHL debut at the new Madison Square Garden in 1925, fans were thrilled by the speed and finesse of the players, especially the flamboyant superstar Howie Morenz. It was a game that might never have been played — if Morenz had not been equally spectacular on the night Rickard and Runyon saw him play a few months earlier.

The Day Howie Morenz Quit Hockey

WHEN I TALK with hockey old-timers, men who remember the early stars of the game, invariably they speak of Howie Morenz. They talk of his lightning speed and his incredible rushes and how he ranks among the top ten players ever to put on skates.

But Morenz's career almost ended before it began. The Morenz family was from Mitchell, Ontario, but when Howie was a teenager the family moved to nearby Stratford. The Stratford hockey team, having heard that young Howie had shown some promise as a high school player in Mitchell, invited him to try out for the local team.

When he arrived at the rink, Howie had only his skates and a stick because his family was too poor to provide him with any additional equipment. In the scrimmage that followed, Howie was roughly handled by the fully equipped Stratford boys. In the dressing room he showed the manager his bruised and bleeding hands. "The other boys hacked at my hands because I have no gloves," he protested. "You won't see me out for your team again." And he walked out into the night.

Morenz was all but forgotten until later in the season when the Stratford club took a beating from archrival Kitchener. The manager, seeking ways to strengthen his team, remembered the kid with no equipment and gave Morenz a call. Would he come and help them out in their return match with Kitchener? The club would even scrape up some gloves, pants, and shin pads for him. Morenz agreed and turned in an outstanding game, beginning a career that would take him right to the peak of professional hockey with the Montreal Canadiens.

Bruins Seek Goalie: Aging Rookie Gets the Job

IN 1971 ROSS BROOKS, a 34-year-old goalie with 13 dreary winters of playing in hockey's minor leagues behind him, was almost ready to give up his dream of making the NHL. It was not only a personal disappointment, but it was unfortunate for another reason: Brooks would have provided the answer to a wonderful new question for trivia buffs. Who was the only Jewish netminder in NHL history?

After all, he had spent the past seven years as a backup goaltender in Providence, playing only when Marcel Paille, the Reds' number one man, was extremely weary or incapacitated. Then, to his consternation, midway through the 1971–72 season, Brooks was handed his outright release by Providence management.

"I was stunned," he said. "I thought about buying a lunch bucket and finding a job, but I still wanted to play hockey more than anything. My wife and I decided to sit down and write a letter to every general manager in every league. It cost us all of eight bucks for paper and stamps and the message was simple — I was out of work and wanted to play.

"Talk about luck. My letter reached Milt Schmidt of the Bruins just when he was seeking a goalie. He

37

called me and signed me and sent me to Oklahoma City. Then it was on to the Boston Braves [a Bruin farm team in the American League] where I shared goalie of the year honors with Dan Bouchard. When Bouchard was drafted by Atlanta, an expansion team, and when Gerry Cheevers, Boston's number one goalie, bolted to the WHA, I got a call from the Bruins and finally found myself in the NHL. I was 36, one of the oldest rookies ever, and while it was no big deal, I became the first Jewish goaltender in league history."

After a decade of playing in the shadow of other netminders, Brooks was determined to make the most of his opportunity. For the next three seasons he played the best hockey of his career. During one stretch, he won 14 consecutive games to equal a team mark set by the legendary Tiny Thompson in 1929–30. By the end of his rookie season he'd compiled an extraordinary record of 16–3–0 with a goals-against average of 2.36. For two more seasons, playing backup to Gilles Gilbert, he was always ready and always reliable. When he retired in 1974, his big league stats were 37–7–6. His career goals-against average was 2.64 — lower than that of two Bruin Hall of Famers, Gerry Cheevers (2.89) and Frankie Brimsek (2.70).

"A lot of people, especially young people, could look at my story and learn something from it," Brooks said after he bowed from the scene with no regrets. "After so many years of people doubting I could play well, so many years of people not knowing I was alive out there, after a lot of perseverance and hard work, I finally achieved my goal and proved myself with the greatest team in hockey."

The Strange Twist That Brought Tony McKegney to the NHL

THE FIRST BLACK PLAYER to reach the NHL was Willie O'Ree, who enjoyed a brief stint with the Boston Bruins, joining them for a two-game trial in 1957–58. He rejoined them in 1960–61, scored four goals in 45 games, went back to the minors, and never resurfaced in the NHL. Mike Marson and Bill Riley joined the Washington Capitals in the seventies, but they, too, didn't stay around long. Marson scored 24 goals in 196 NHL games, Riley 31 in 139 games.

Clearly Tony McKegney from Sarnia, Ontario, stands out as the first black player to become a prolific NHL scorer — collecting 320 goals in a career that embraced 912 NHL games and saw him perform with eight different teams, including the Buffalo Sabres where he began his NHL career in October 1978.

But prior to that, in the spring of 1978, he became the first hockey player to be released from a pro contract — for racial reasons. It happened when John Bassett, owner of the Birmingham Bulls of the World Hockey Association, persuaded McKegney, a blue-chip prospect in junior hockey, to sign a contract with his Bulls. Bassett promised McKegney he wouldn't have to spend any time in the minor leagues and that he would play on a line with Ken Linesman, his centerman from junior hockey days in Kingston, Ontario. The deal appealed to McKegney. Deciding not to wait for the NHL draft to find out which club would select him, he signed a lucrative contract with Bassett.

A few days later, to McKegney's consternation,

39

Bassett announced that he was releasing the young star from his Birmingham contract. The announcement of McKegney's signing had triggered an angry reaction from racists in Birmingham. Several season ticket holders threatened to cancel their tickets to Bulls games if a black player joined the team. Bassett reluctantly let McKegney go, and when the NHL draft was held that June, the Buffalo Sabres made McKegney their number one choice.

Bassett later apologized to the citizens of Birmingham, claiming he had "overreacted" to a very few complaints.

"The Birmingham situation came as a major surprise to me," McKegney told hockey writer Frank Orr of the *Toronto Star.* "I'd never run into anything like that in my life."

Tony McKegney, the first black player to become an NHL star.
(Robert B. Shaver)

40

Another oddity in McKegney's background is that he had two hockey playing brothers — one white and one black. His parents, Larry and Cathy McKegney of Sarnia, had six children, three of whom were adopted. Tony's brother Ian, who is white, played in the Chicago chain, and his brother Mike, who is black, played in the American Hockey League and in Europe.

PART

BIZARRE BUSINESS

Keep Your Eye on Bobby's Slapshot

IN THE SIXTIES Bobby Hull of the Chicago Blackhawks was hockey's biggest gunner. With a powerful slapshot that was timed at over 100 miles per hour, Bobby terrorized opposing goaltenders. In 1965–66 he scored a record-breaking 54 goals and added 43 assists to win his third Art Ross Trophy as NHL scoring champion. A year later, in the Stanley Cup playoffs against Toronto, Leaf executive Harold Ballard proclaimed, "If we can stop Hull and his bleeping slapshot, we can win this series."

Ballard never figured he would play a personal role in stopping one of Hull's slapshots, but that was what happened midway through the series. During the warm-up before a game at Maple Leaf Gardens, Hull unleashed a slapshot that soared much higher than he intended. It flew over the protective glass and smashed into the face of Ballard, who was occupying his private box at the Gardens' north end. The bones in Ballard's nose were crunched in four places, his glasses were shattered, and blood flowed freely all over his expensive suit.

Pal Hal was rushed to the Gardens' medical clinic where team doctors treated his injury. By then both of his eyes were swollen almost shut, and the skin around them was beginning to change color. Just then, through the open door, he saw Hull and the Blackhawks leave their dressing room and begin to make their way toward the ice.

Ballard bolted from the table, grabbed Hull's arm as he passed by, and pulled him into the clinic. "Get a photographer in here quick!" he ordered one of his staff. "I want to get a picture of Bobby and me

45

The Golden Jet at the height of his popularity in the mid-sixties. (Robert C. Ragsdale)

together. It'll make the front page of every paper tomorrow."

Hull was willing to oblige, but Billy Reay, his coach, who suddenly appeared at the door, had other ideas. "Get the hell out on the ice, Bobby," Reay barked. "This is no time for picture taking."

It took Bobby a few seconds to figure out why his coach reacted the way he did. Then he remembered. Years earlier Reay had been fired by Ballard and the Leafs. Obviously he had a long memory and was in no mood to do Ballard any favors.

Dinny "Dollar Bill" Dinsmore

IN 1930 MANAGER DUNC MUNRO of the Montreal Maroons said he was ready to believe in Santa Claus and the tooth fairy after a conversation with chunky defenseman Charlie "Dinny" Dinsmore. Dinsmore, a heavily built little player who had been a popular Maroon until the 1928–29 season, asked manager Munro if he could make a comeback — for the princely sum of a dollar a year.

Munro instantly agreed. How often does a man-

46

ager get an opportunity to sign a proven big leaguer for the price of a good cigar? Dinsmore, known as "the pest" for his ability to shadow opposing scoring stars, was only 27 years old. He had retired a few months earlier to become a bond salesman, but the lure of the game was strong. So he became the first player in history to sign a contract for a dollar.

Alas, Dinny failed to become the bargain Munro hoped he would be. His skills had faded and he was quickly released.

"I thought I could make a defenseman out of him," Munro said, "but he couldn't handle the position. But hey, it only cost me a buck to find out."

A Bonus in Buffalo

A LITTLE-KNOWN STORY in Buffalo Sabre hockey history concerns a player named Paul McIntosh. He didn't stay around long, but when Floyd Smith was coaching there, McIntosh figured in a most unusual incident. He had played in 39 games for Buffalo one season and his contract called for a $15,000 bonus if he took part in 40 games. Smith had orders from GM Punch Imlach to let McIntosh dress for game number 40, but under no circumstances was he to get any ice time.

With the season just about over, Imlach figured to save his club 15 grand if McIntosh didn't play. But late in the game the Sabre players decided to take matters into their own hands. With two minutes to play, three or four Sabres grabbed McIntosh and, despite his protests, physically threw him onto the ice while the team was changing lines "on the fly." There was nothing Smith or Imlach could

47

do. The few seconds McIntosh played were enough to count as an "official" appearance, and Imlach grudgingly awarded McIntosh his bonus. He even played him in two more games, giving McIntosh a chance to score his first goal of the season. But McIntosh failed to produce.

King Clancy Gets Starched

ONE OF HOCKEY'S greatest storytellers was the late Hall of Famer King Clancy, former star defenseman with the Toronto Maple Leafs and, prior to that, the Ottawa Senators. One day I asked Clancy to tell me about hockey's renowned tough guy of the twenties — Sprague Cleghorn.

"Sprague was an awesome competitor in the NHL," King said. "He broke his leg in a game one year and was so frustrated at being sidelined that he hauled off and struck his wife with his crutch. The story made all the papers when his wife took him to court. And he was always getting into disputes with his coaches and other players in the league — some of them on his own team.

"I remember in 1923 when he played for Montreal and cross-checked Boston's Lionel Hitchman dizzy in a playoff game. Cleghorn's manager, Leo Dandurand, was so repelled that he didn't wait for the league to discipline his star. He suspended Cleghorn himself because of his violent behavior on the ice. His own player!

"When I was a rookie with the Ottawa Senators, I got cute with Cleghorn one night, and boy, did I suffer the consequences. He was lugging the puck up the ice and I was right behind him, trying to catch up.

48

When I realized I wasn't going to overtake him, I yelled, 'Sprague, drop the puck!' Well, he thought I was a teammate calling for a pass, and without looking back, he dropped the puck right onto my stick.

"As I wheeled around and led a return rush, the Ottawa fans howled with laughter. But Cleghorn did a slow burn and his cheeks turned beet red. No player likes being humiliated like that, especially by a rookie, and Cleghorn was no exception. He glared at me but did nothing at the time. But when the period ended and the players were leaving the ice — we all left by the same exit in those days — I heard someone behind me say, 'Oh, King!' I turned around, and that's when every light in the rink went out. Cleghorn had starched me. When I finally opened my eyes, the trainer was throwing water in my face and there was a priest bending over me.

"That gave me a start. I thought I was getting the last rites. I was told later that when my teammates tried to get at Sprague, he fended them off with his stick and insisted, 'Honest, fellows, all I said to King was that he had the makings of a great little hockey player. And then I gave him a friendly pat on the head.'

"I'll say this. It's the only pat on the head I ever heard of that required a bucket of water to revive a fellow and brought a Catholic priest on the run."

Some Teams Will Do Anything to Win

MANY YEARS AGO two small towns in Ontario developed a fierce hockey rivalry. Whenever Brantford played Preston, fan

49

interest was at a peak. Winning was so important to the rivals that on at least one occasion an attempt was made to bribe the referee. Midway through one bitterly fought game, referee Jimmy Fraser was offered $10 if he would make sure Brantford won. When he declined the money and Preston squeezed out a one-goal victory, Fraser was approached again. This time he was offered $15 if he would report to the Ontario Hockey Association that the winning goal was scored after the expiration of time.

In 1895 in Quebec City, Ottawa edged Quebec 3–2 one night and the crowd became very hostile toward the referee, a man named Hamilton. After the game, a number of fans chased Hamilton and captured him just as he was about to board a train for Montreal. They dragged him back to the arena and, twisting his arm, tried to coerce him into declaring the match a draw. Fortunately police arrived just in time to rescue the badly shaken official and escort him back to the train station, from whence he happily fled the city.

The Cup Winners Promised to Double the Score

IN THE SPRING OF 1908 the Montreal Wanderers were the hottest team in hockey. Over the previous three seasons they had won 27 league games and lost only three. In the 1907 season they had established a record that has never been matched, going undefeated and *averaging* over 10 goals per game. In one game they routed the Montreal Vics 16–3, and in two outings against the Shamrocks they won by 18–5 and 16–5. Ernie Russell, their top scorer, compiled the staggering record of 42 goals in the nine games he played — an average of over four goals per game.

They were just as formidable in the annual chase for the Stanley Cup in those years, winning the trophy in three straight seasons. In 1908 they walloped Ottawa 9–3 and 13–1 in one Stanley Cup series. They immediately accepted a challenge from the Winnipeg Maple Leafs and crushed the westerners by scores of 11–5 and 9–3.

That triumph seemed like a fitting end to a hugely successful season. But just as the Wanderers were preparing to put their skates away, they were handed a third Stanley Cup challenge — this time from the Toronto Maple Leafs, champions of the Trolley League, the first outright professional league in Canada. The Trolley League was so named because teams traveled by electric trolley between games in Ontario hockey hotbeds like Toronto, Brantford, Guelph, and Berlin (later renamed Kitchener).

But the arrogant Wanderers treated the Maple Leaf challenge as a joke. "Toronto doesn't have a chance against us," a Wanderer spokesman told reporters. "If the Cup trustees order us to play a two-game series against Toronto, it would be a travesty. We'd more than double the score against them. And who would show up for a boring second game? So let's make it a one-game affair and get the season over with." The Cup trustees agreed, and the Toronto boys were given only one chance against the mighty Wanderers.

The game was played in Montreal on March 14, 1908, and the Wanderer fans who turned out bet huge sums that their heroes would double the score on the Maple Leafs, even though the visitors had young Newsy Lalonde in their lineup. Lalonde had been the leading scorer in the Trolley League with 29 goals in nine games.

The Stanley Cup game seesawed back and forth and was tied four times. Montrealers exhorted the champions to pick up the pace, for they were in grave danger of losing their wagers. Some of the fans, during a halt in play, motioned three or four Wanderer players, including goaltender Riley Hern, over to the side boards. "You promised to double the score on these chaps," they shouted. "If you pull up your socks and do it, there'll be some bonus money for you to divide up after the game."

While the players were listening to these enticements, one of the strangest goals in Stanley Cup history was scored. The referee, ignoring the distraction at rinkside, dropped the puck at center ice, and Lalonde fired it quickly toward the Wanderer net. His aim was true and the disk sailed past the opposing players, who scrambled back too late to prevent the goal. However, Lalonde's empty-net goal so fired up the champions that they stormed back with two goals of their own and won the game by a 6–4 score.

The Wanderers retained the Stanley Cup, but their supporters lost a bundle when the score wasn't doubled. The Toronto boys, on the other hand, had been in on the wagering and returned with a pot of $2,500 to divide among themselves — a small fortune in that era.

52

Let's Get the Puck Out of Here

THE BOSTON BRUINS and the New York Americans played a pair of unique games during the 1931–32 season. On December 8, 1931, in Boston the Americans shot the puck down the ice at every opportunity. Although boring to the fans, it was a great way to take the pressure off while playing a superior team. Since no rules had yet been devised to prevent "icing the puck," the Bruins spent most of the evening chasing the disk back into their own zone. That night it happened 61 times, leaving the Boston players frustrated and their fans furious.

Bruins owner Charles Adams vowed to get even. On January 3, 1932, in a game played on New York ice, Boston "iced the puck" 87 times. The two games rank as perhaps the most boring ever played. Some of the NHL owners felt that Adams should have been fined up to $10,000 for retaliation, but NHL president Frank Calder said no. Under the existing rules his players had every right to do what they did. Then Calder immediately introduced a rule designed to curb icing the puck, one that prevented a recurrence of the farce.

A Hockey Riot in Britain

IN 1937 LONDON, ENGLAND, was the site of the world amateur hockey championships, and British fans were wildly excited about the prospects of a gold medal for their team. The British squad, stacked with Canadians born in

Great Britain, had gone through the tournament without surrendering a single goal. Jimmy Foster, a sturdy goalkeeper formerly with the Moncton Hawks, had chalked up seven shutouts in seven games — a remarkable feat — and a victory over Canada in the semifinal game would all but ensure the world title for Britain.

The big game, played at Harringay Arena, attracted over 10,000 fans. They looked on in dismay as Canada's Allan Cup champions, the Kimberley, B.C., Dynamiters, beat Foster for three goals and won 3–0. The angry mob decided at game's end that the referee was to blame, and M. Poplemont of Belgium fled for his life at the final buzzer. He was showered with garbage — tin cans, beer bottles, apples, and oranges — as he made a hasty exit. Several youths chased him, and he was forced to seek sanctuary in a nearby restaurant under police protection.

Back at the arena the mob turned on the Canadian players, and several might have been beaten up but for the intervention of 50 sailors from the Canadian sloop *Frazer*. They surrounded the hockey players and fought off the assaults of the fans, who accused the Dynamiters of dirty tactics.

Frustrated at being unable to pummel the players, the fans then roughed up several attendants and arena employees and smashed countless windows in the building. The riot rocked the arena for close to an hour and was finally stopped by an enterprising band leader. He assembled his musicians, most of whom were changing into street clothes in a dressing room, and led them in a rendition of "God Save the King."

The rampaging throng stood stock-still for a moment, then slowly began removing their hats. A few even sang the anthem. When the last strains died away, everybody was so calm that the arena was cleared in a matter of minutes.

The riot was called the worst in many years in British sport. The Kimberley boys must have been rattled by the experience, because they were hard-pressed to edge Switzerland 2–1 in overtime in their final game. They captured the world crown with eight straight victories, six of them shutouts. England won 5–0 over Germany (a seventh shutout for Jimmy Foster) to take the runner-up position.

The Goalie's Release Was Forged

IN 1906 GOALIE HENRI MENARD of the Montreal Wanderers filled his daytime hours enrolled as a student at the University of Laval. One day a stranger handed him a letter. It read: "Dear Mr. Menard. As the Wanderers have been able to obtain a goalie with outstanding credentials, we will not require your services in the game tonight against the Shamrocks. Thank you for your past efforts on our behalf. [Signed] James Strachan, President."

That evening the young netminder entered the arena moments before game time and was surprised to find an anxious band of Wanderers relieved to see him. "Get dressed!" they demanded. "Why are you so late? Where have you been?"

"But I'm not playing tonight," he told them. "I was released today. I have the letter of dismissal in my pocket."

Mr. Strachan, the club president, stepped forward.

"Let me see this letter," he demanded. After scanning the document, he cried, "This is a forgery. That's not my signature. Some despicable rascal, obviously a Shamrock supporter, tried to keep you out of the game tonight."

Menard hastily suited up and played a solid game for the Wanderers in their victory over the Shamrocks. Meanwhile news of the forged letter swept through Montreal hockey circles. A reporter wrote: "Great indignation was expressed over the meanness of the artifice. Two detectives have been hired to investigate the forgery."

But the culprit was never discovered, even though a reward of $25 was posted for his arrest and conviction.

Watch Out for the Bandstand!

DURING THE SEASON OF 1885–86, the first college game in Kingston, Ontario, was played between Queen's University and the Royal Military College. The site of the game was in an open-air rink in Kingston harbor, where many games of shinny had been played over the years.

The cadets from the Royal Military College ordered new sticks from Halifax for the big match, sticks made out of small planed-down trees with the curved roots carved into blades. The Queen's players were green with envy when the new sticks arrived, and they insisted on being supplied with a half dozen, as well — otherwise they might not show up for the game.

The most bizarre feature of this historic matchup was a bandstand — right in the middle of the ice.

56

Out of the bandstand rose an electric light standard. Strangely none of the players complained about this hazard, even though the opposing goalies couldn't see what was happening on the far side of the structure.

The play was very close, but in the final few minutes the bandstand turned the tide in favor of Queen's. Their star player, Lennox Irving, swept around the bandstand and looked up to make his shot on goal. Incredibly the RMC net was empty. Off to the side the rival goalie and one of his point men were sitting in a snowbank. The point man was struggling to strap on the goalie's skate, which had slipped from his foot. They had relied on having a few seconds to secure the blade to the boot because the play had moved into the Queen's zone moments earlier.

Now, with Irving racing toward them, the cadets scrambled back onto the ice. But they were too late. Irving's shot found the empty goal. If the cadets thought of registering a protest, it wouldn't have done them much good, for there was no goal judge in this game and no referee. The teams hadn't thought there was any need for outside help. They abided by the rules they had set themselves and everybody agreed that Queen's had won an exciting victory.

A Special Train for Charlie

IN 1902 A MONTREAL TEAM left for Ottawa and a big game with the Senators. But there was one major problem: Montreal's star player, Charlie Liffiton, was unable to get off work in time to catch

57

the train and would have to be left behind. Montreal officials huddled and agreed their chances against Ottawa were slim without Liffiton. So they chartered a special train for the player.

When Liffiton was released from work, he raced to the station and hopped aboard the "special." Just Charlie, alone in a car, while up front the engineer and the fireman pushed the train to breakneck speeds. The train left Montreal at 6:20 p.m. and arrived in Ottawa at 8:40 — 20 minutes ahead of game time. A horse-drawn sleigh got the star player to the arena in time to throw on his uniform and be ready for the opening whistle. In order to have Liffiton in the Montreal lineup, team officials paid $114 to the CPR for the special train.

Was it worth it? Indeed it was, for Liffiton, who was averaging a goal a game, paced Montreal to a 4–2 victory.

The Strange Entry Draft of 1974

TODAY THE ANNUAL NHL entry draft is a showcase event, with future stars parading to the teams drafting them and proudly donning team jerseys while flashbulbs pop and a nationwide TV audience looks on. Let a Mario Lemieux or an Eric Lindros show the least reluctance to embrace the drafting club and instant headlines are created.

So it is hard to believe that the annual draft of teenage talent was once conducted in secret, with all the choices being made over the telephone. In 1974 the hush-hush draft was held behind closed doors because of increasing competition for young players by the World Hockey Association.

Some oddities of that draft:

- While it was touted as a secret draft, there were some major leaks. Reporters seemed to know all about the selections — and announced them to the public — almost before they were made.
- Washington, an expansion team, made 20-year-old defenseman Greg Joly the number one choice after Pat Price, the player the Capitals really wanted, skipped to the WHA.
- The Montreal Canadiens, thanks to some shrewd wheeling and dealing by Sam Pollock, owned no less than five draft choices in the first round. After Greg Joly (Washington), Wilf Paiement (Kansas City), Rick Hampton (California), and Clark Gillies (Islanders) were selected, the Canadiens took Cam Connor (5th). They also acquired Doug Risebrough (7th), Rick Chartraw (10th), Mario Tremblay (12th), and Gord McTavish (17th).
- The telephone draft was found to be incredibly slow, spanning three days.
- The Buffalo Sabres contributed the most amusing twist. General manager Punch Imlach selected a little-known Japanese star, Taro Tsujimoto, in the 12th round. Tsujimoto was described as a five-foot-eight, 180-pound center from the Tokyo Katanas. It marked the first time an Asian player had been drafted, *The Hockey News*

reported. Weeks went by before Imlach confessed it was all a joke. He had plucked Tsujimoto's name from the Buffalo telephone book. No such hockey player existed. "I just wanted to add a little fun to those dreary proceedings," Imlach said.

Waiting in Wetaskiwin

IN 1948–49 ROY BENTLEY (one of the brothers in the famous Bentley clan from Delisle, Saskatchewan) was coaching the Wetaskiwin Canadians in the northern Alberta Junior Hockey League. Wetaskiwin was little more than a dot on a prairie map, but hockey was a serious business there. Many of the players were imports, and the club had the backing of the NHL's Chicago Blackhawks.

In the league finals Wetaskiwin met the Edmonton Athletic Club "We always had troubles with Edmonton, and that playoff year was no exception," Bentley said. Sure enough, Edmonton won the first two games and the series moved south to Wetaskiwin.

That was when Bentley decided to make full use of home ice advantage and a supportive crowd. Before the start of the first period he kept the Wetaskiwin players in their dressing room an abnormally long time. This ruse allowed the hometown fans a chance to verbally abuse the visitors while they skated in lazy circles around the ice.

Before the second period Bentley's boys stayed in their room even longer, and once again the Ed-

60

monton players on the ice were booed and harassed unmercifully. But Bentley's strategy went awry before the third period got under way. The Edmonton players decided to give the Canadians and their fans a taste of their own medicine. Clarence Moher, the Edmonton coach, ordered his players to stay put. They were not to step outside their dressing room until they heard the home team clomping down the corridor toward the ice. And the waiting game was on. The Wetaskiwin players remained behind their dressing room door, while across the hall the Edmonton players waited them out. Players on both teams chewed their gum, sucked on oranges, and waited some more.

The intermission stretched into 10, 15, then 20 minutes. An angry referee and his linesmen banged on both doors and ordered the clubs back onto the ice. The players ignored them.

Occasionally a player would peek through a small hole in the door to see if the other club had budged. "I opened the door a crack and peeked out once," Bentley recalled, "and there was Clarence Moher peeking back at me. Looked like he was determined to sit there all night if necessary."

Finally the referee said, "That's it, boys! There'll be no more hockey tonight." And he called the third period off. The players, no doubt feeling a bit foolish, slowly shed their uniforms and showered while the fans who jammed the arena were left wondering what in blazes had occurred behind the scenes to cause the game to be canceled.

Both coaches were suspended for promoting such ridiculous stalling tactics. Incidentally Edmonton went on to win the series.

61

Grab a Stick, Governor!

THERE WAS A MAJOR SURPRISE when the World Hockey Association held its first player draft in 1972. The Minnesota Fighting Saints, even though they had no hope of landing him, drafted Minnesota Governor Wendell Anderson. Actually the choice wasn't as ridiculous as it appears. Anderson was a key player in the 1956 U.S. Olympic hockey team, silver medalists at the Games held in Cortina, Italy.

Fans Say the Darnedest Things

THE MONTREAL MAROONS once had a Jewish player named Sammy Rothschild who gained a reputation as a keen businessman. Skating at top speed toward a loose puck one night, Rothschild skidded to a stop when he reached the spot on the ice where the puck was resting. He hovered over it, hesitating as he looked around for a place to play it. His procrastination prompted a fan to lean over the boards and yell, "Grab it, Sam! It's a bargain."

When Gordie Howe joined the Houston Aeros of the WHA, he was approached by a fan who was about to see his first big league hockey game. "Say, Gordie," he drawled, "how much air is there in that little old puck?"

Referee Red Storey was working a game during the forties when a lady fan shouted at him during a halt in play, "Hey, Storey, you're a big, strong guy. How come you ain't in the army?"

Red took one look at her and replied, "For the

same reason you ain't in the Folies Bergère, lady —
physically unfit!"

A Behind-the-Scenes Battle for the Canada Cup

CANADA HAS AN IMPRESSIVE RECORD in
Canada Cup play, dating back to 1976. Team
Canada has won four of five championships
with the only blot on the record an 8–1 pummeling
administered by the Soviets in the 1981 championship game. That was the year the Soviets learned
that winning the sparkling trophy is one thing —
keeping it is another.

When the teams left the Montreal Forum that
September night, the Soviets packed the Canada
Cup into a hockey bag and were hurrying for their
bus when they were intercepted by tournament
chairman Alan Eagleson.

*Alan Eagleson, Canadian
hockey's international
impresario.*

"What's in the bag?" Eagleson asked Soviet official Valentin Sytch.

When Sytch replied, "None of your business," or some similar retort in the Russian language, Eagleson made a grab for the bag.

"You buggers, you've got the Cup in there. Now hand it over!"

While Eagleson clutched one end of the bag, Sytch latched onto the other end. The two men pushed and pulled, arguing all the while, and finally Eagleson's strength won out. He threw open the bag and collared the Cup.

"It's the Canada Cup," he shouted as he hustled the trophy away, leaving the Soviet delegation gnashing their teeth. "That means it stays in Canada."

And it always has.

Playboy Seeks Hockey Player for Nude Layout

WHO WOULD HAVE THOUGHT that *Playboy,* the men's magazine, would offer a hockey player $75,000 to appear nude in the publication? Yet it happened in 1992.

The hockey player is the young female player Manon Rheaume, who made headlines by playing in goal with the Trois-Rivières Draveurs, a Junior A team in the Province of Quebec. Manon became the first woman to play as high as the Junior A level. In November 1991 she was called off the bench in the second period of a game between Trois-Rivières and the Granby Bisons. She played 20 minutes, allowed three goals on 10 shots, and left the game

64

when she was cut for three stitches by a slapshot to the face mask.

Rheaume used a different dressing room and showered away from the other players. "When the players first saw me at tryout camp, they were amused," she said. "But in no time they stopped treating me like a girl."

A few weeks later she turned down a $75,000 offer from *Playboy* to pose nude in a future issue of the magazine. "I wouldn't do that for a million dollars," the attractive young goaltender insisted.

Rheaume went on to become the first female player to play for a professional hockey team, signing with the Atlanta Knights of the International Hockey League. Prior to the 1992–93 season she also tended goal briefly in an exhibition game for the Tampa Bay Lightning.

A Sponsorship Scandal in Germany

IN 1986–87 THE ISERLOHN TEAM in the West German Federal League was in financial difficulties. Two players with NHL experience, Slava Duris (Toronto) and Jaroslav Pouzar (Edmonton), discovered that collecting paychecks from the team owner, Hans Weissenbach, was tougher than stopping a three-on-one.

"There were arguments over money all the time," Duris said. "And pretty soon he wasn't paying us anything at all. So Pouzar and I said, 'That's it. We won't be back for the next game.' And we stayed away. It wasn't long before the owner came around and gave us a few bills — just enough to keep us from bolting — but we could tell the situation was grave and the team might fold at any moment."

The City of Iserlohn wanted to save the franchise. Civic officials offered to bankroll the team, but Weissenbach said no. He would find a new sponsor for his club, one with plenty of ready cash. And he did.

An important source of income for European clubs is the sale of advertising space on team uniforms. The smooth-talking Weissenbach sold space on two sets of uniforms. One set was used in the pregame warm-up and a second set was used during the game itself. After the warm-up before their next game, when the Iserlohn players reached the dressing room, they were handed game jerseys with the words "Green Book" written across the front.

Green Book! Duris and Pouzar knew what that meant. Surely they weren't going to be a skating advertisement for the infamous book written by Moammar Khaddafy, advocate of terrorism.

During the game, the players found themselves getting more attention than they had ever received before. Still photographers and television cameras followed their movements on the ice and, within hours, the scandalous advertising on their jerseys created a furor throughout the league. The West German Hockey Association, when it discovered that Weissenbach was paying off his considerable debts with a wad of bills acquired from Khaddafy, held an emergency meeting and voted to turf Iserlohn out of the circuit.

The players couldn't wait to ditch those god-awful jerseys and get out of town. Duris signed on with Landshut and Pouzar was acquired by Rosenheim. In both places, they reported, the uni-

66

forms were much more attractive. And the pay-checks much more frequent.

A Dummy in Goal

OME HOCKEY PEOPLE, including several prominent players who chose the position, say a fellow has to be crazy to play in goal. Either that or he has to be a real dummy. But only once in NHL history has a dummy been between the pipes.

Many decades ago the Chicago Blackhawks' eccentric owner Major Frederic McLaughlin decided his team needed a second goaltender, one who would be good company for All-Star netminder Charlie Gardiner. McLaughlin wanted a practice goalie only, one who had no fear of shooting drills, one who never complained, and best of all, one who never had to be paid. Presto! He invented hockey's first dummy.

Chicago goalie Charlie Gardiner. Certainly no dummy. (Hockey Hall of Fame)

67

McLaughlin had a member of his staff stuff bags full of straw into a scarecrow-shaped figure roughly resembling a goalie. When the job was done, the dummy was hauled across the ice and strung up in the center of the goal net. While All-Star goalie Charlie Gardiner tended goal in practice at one end of the ice, the dummy defended the opposite goal. Chicago players took their hardest shots at the chunky figure, hoping to knock the stuffing out of the latest addition to their roster.

For the next few days Gardiner heard comments in the dressing room like: "That dummy's lookin' better every day. He never complains about us shootin' high or yaps at us for not clearin' the puck. He's a lot smarter than our other guy and better lookin', too. He deserves a start, don't you think? In fact, I hear the owner's signed the dummy long-term and wants to send our other guy to the minors."

The other guy — Gardiner — took the ribbing in stride for a few days. Then he ended the dummy experiment once and for all. After practice one day, he hauled the dummy into the dressing room, flopped him onto the rubbing table, and said to the trainer, "Give this poor kid a rubdown, will you? He's falling to pieces out there. Then find some clothes for him, give him a few bucks for a beer and a sandwich, and get him the hell out of here."

Ottawa Acquired an All-Star Player — For Nothing

TOMMY GORMAN, who once guided the Chicago Blackhawks and the Montreal Maroons to successive Stanley Cups, was managing

68

the Ottawa club in 1919 and he needed defensive help. The player he coveted was rugged Sprague Cleghorn, a star performer with the Montreal Wanderers.

When the league managers gathered in Montreal for a preseason meeting, Gorman took Wanderers manager Sam Lichtenhein aside and casually mentioned that he was somewhat interested in Cleghorn.

"You know he broke his leg in an auto accident last summer?" Lichtenhein asked.

"Yes, I know about that mishap," Gorman replied.

"And you know he more or less skipped out of the hospital and broke his other leg?" Lichtenhein added.

"My goodness, two broken legs," Gorman said. "That doesn't auger well."

"Then his wife swore out a warrant for his arrest. So he's got some personal problems, too."

"Oh, my," Gorman said.

"The guy is jinxed," Lichtenhein snorted. "He's a write-off. You want him, you can have him. He'll never play hockey again."

"I'm probably making a big mistake, but I'll take him," Gorman said. "How much?"

"Nothin'," Lichtenhein said. "I said you could have him. He's not worth anything."

So Sprague Cleghorn's name was quietly placed on the Ottawa reserve list.

Early in December, on the eve of the new NHL season, Gorman received a phone call from Montreal. It was Sprague Cleghorn.

"I think my legs have healed perfectly," he said. "My wife and I have solved our problems and I'm anxious to play hockey again, especially for you."

It cost Gorman only $8.50 — the price of two train tickets — to bring Cleghorn and his wife from Montreal to Ottawa. When Cleghorn stepped on the ice the next day, his legs were perfect. That season he went on to become the most brilliant defenseman in the NHL.

Smith Goes on Rampage in 1911 Game

STAR FORWARD HARRY SMITH'S last game in the Timiskaming League in Northern Ontario was a memorable one. A write-up in the Cobalt newspaper on Monday, January 16, 1911, featured the headline: "Harry Smith under Arrest. Cobalt Player Struck Opponents and Felled Referee. Smashed Teeth and Broke Noses in Haileybury Match."

Harry Smith, center of the Cobalt team, played his last game of hockey in this section last night when near the close of the first half of the game against Haileybury, two policemen walked onto the ice and nabbed him for deliberate rough work. Harry was escorted to the cells but was subsequently let out on bail.

In the first ten minutes of the game little rough work was done, but shortly afterwards Smith hit Johnston with the blade of his stick, breaking Johnston's nose, for which Smith spent five minutes on the fence. When he came back, he cut Morrison on the lip and loosened two teeth. He then struck at Skene Ronan and got another five

70

minutes. He had just got on the ice again when Con Corbeau started down with the puck and Harry chopped him.

George Gwynne of Liskeard, the referee, skated over and called Smith to the penalty box. While Gwynne was going to the side, Smith skated up behind him, and swinging his stick like an axe, struck the referee with the blade over the side of the face. This was too much for the crowd, and Chief Miller and PC Collins arrested Smith on the spot.

Referee Gwynne received two bad cuts on the face and above his eye as well as two broken teeth.

The executive of the league will probably forbid Smith from ever playing again.

During the following week, another write-up appeared:

Twenty-five dollars and costs was the fine meted out to Harry Smith, the Cobalt hockey player, by Magistrate Atkinson as a result of Smith's rampage during the hockey game on Friday night. In addition Smith received a severe lecture from the judge. The information was laid by Chief Miller, referee Gwynne not caring to lay information. The Magistrate told Smith that if Gwynne had laid the charge or even been present the defendant would have been given a lengthy prison term.

Just as the sentence was announced, the referee came rushing into the courtroom to lay the charge.

But it was too late. Smith was allowed to go free after paying his fine.

And they say modern hockey is violent.

He Played for One Club While Coaching Another

THERE WERE SOME mighty strange goings-on in English hockey during the thirties. In 1937 Len Burrage, a defenseman from Winnipeg, made history by playing for one club while coaching another — in the same league.

The British Ice Hockey Association saw nothing unusual in Burrage holding down a defense position with Harringay while toiling as coach of the Manchester Rapids, another member of the 11-team league.

But there was one date on the schedule that troubled the association. On March 2 Harringay was pitted against Manchester. Would Burrage act as player or coach? The fans submitted all kinds of suggestions. One thought he should play a period for each team and then coach in the third period. Another thought his role should be decided by a coin flip. A third thought he should take a neutral position and referee the game. Yet another suggested he stay at home and read a good book.

As it turned out, the association made the decision for Burrage. After a vote was taken, Burrage was ordered to play in the game because he had joined Harringay before accepting the coaching position with Manchester.

That same year another player in the British

72

league had a similar problem. Baron Richard Von Trauttenberg, who played with Streatham, journeyed with his team on a tour of Europe. But when Streatham got to Vienna, Von Trauttenberg deserted his club and joined the opposing team. Seems he had recently been named captain of the Austrian national team and felt honor-bound to play at least one game for his country's representatives.

Pro Football in a Hockey Rink

THE CHAMPIONSHIP of a professional football league was once decided in a hockey rink. On December 18, 1932, a raging blizzard swept over the city of Chicago, site of the football game that would end the U.S. pro season.

As temperatures dropped and snow piled up on the gridiron, officials decided to play the game in the Chicago Stadium, hockey home of the Chicago Blackhawks. Seats were moved back, several inches of dirt were spread over the floor of the arena, and 11,000 fans turned out to witness the unique sports event between the Chicago Bears and the Portsmouth Spartans.

Because the "field" was a mere 80 yards long, every time a team crossed midfield it was penalized 20 yards. The star of the Portsmouth team didn't play because of a job commitment. He left the team to become basketball coach at Colorado College. And the only touchdown was scored on a pass from Bronko Nagurski to Red Grange — two of the greatest players ever. The strange contest was the first championship game of the new National Football League.

The Missing Choppers

A MINOR MYSTERY was part of the 1981 All-Star game played in Los Angeles. But it was quickly solved before anyone even thought of calling Columbo, the famous Hollywood detective.

While the teams were being introduced, overzealous maintenance employees entered the team dressing room with brooms, vacuums, and dustpans. Their orders were clear: keep the rooms spotless. Dutifully they swept up every scrap of paper and tape — and every paper cup. What they failed to notice in one of those paper cups were Bill Barber's false teeth.

During the first intermission, when the Philadelphia Flyer star reached his place in the dressing room, to his horror he noticed the cup — and his teeth — were missing. At first he thought it was a practical joke. Hadn't Guy Lapointe of Montreal once gathered up his teammates' dentures from similar paper cups and mailed them back to the Montreal Forum — while the Habs were on an extended road trip? And hadn't Toronto's George Armstrong once switched teammate Johnny Bower's teeth with a similar-looking set, claiming later that he had picked up the substitute dentures from an undertaker?

But this was no joke. Barber's teeth had simply vanished.

A frantic search was quickly organized. All maintenance workers were assembled and ordered to find the missing dentures — or else. Searchers spent the second period sorting through a ton of garbage and looking into a thousand paper cups.

74

Still no choppers. The search went on through the final period, and just when everyone was beginning to despair, a young hero-to-be, pawing through the contents of a garbage can he had overturned, flipped over a paper cup, looked inside, and smiled. Smiling back at him were Barber's dentures.

The discovery came in the nick of time. Barber was runner-up to Mike Liut as MVP of the game, and he came in for plenty of attention in the postgame press conference. The smile he gave all the cameramen was one of happiness — and relief.

Ivan Lost His Nose

WHEN IVAN MATULIK left his native Czechoslovakia to join the Halifax Citadels of the American Hockey League, he thought he was prepared for anything: a new lifestyle, initiations, an 80-game schedule, long bus rides, fast foods — the works.

One thing he hadn't planned on was losing part of his nose. The accident occurred during the 1991–92 season on a Halifax road trip, and it happened so quickly that Ivan isn't quite sure how it transpired. During the play, players collided. A skate blade arced past Ivan's face and neatly sliced off part of his nose.

Blood flowed as he left the ice to be given immediate attention by the team trainer and doctors. He was told part of his nose was missing. But could it be found? Could it be reattached?

By this time the period was over and the Zamboni was circling the ice. It had already passed over the area of the ice where the accident had occurred.

75

The missing tip of Ivan's nose must be inside the machine, mixed in with a pile of slush and snow.

When the Zamboni dumped its chilly load, the search began. It was like looking for a needle in a haystack. But the searchers were rewarded when one of them held up a pink piece of flesh.

Ivan Matulik and the tip of his nose were rushed to hospital where a surgeon skillfully reattached it. Ivan was told by doctors that operations of this type were often quite successful. It was fortunate, he was told, that the nose tip had been surrounded by ice and snow.

Today Ivan's nose looks and feels perfectly normal. He is thankful he got prompt medical attention and he knows now that a hockey player has to be prepared for anything, even the loss of part of his anatomy.

PART

AUTOCRATS AND AVATARS OF THE ARENA

Ballard Made Leaf Fans Boil

WHEN HAROLD BALLARD ran the Toronto Maple Leaf franchise in the seventies and eighties, he was constantly making headlines with his outrageous behavior and comments. Here are several things he did or said that caused many to call him names like "tyrant," "chauvinist," "racist," and "boor."

- Guesting on *As It Happens,* a CBC radio show, he called popular broadcaster Barbara Frum "a dumb broad," told her to "shut up," and further shocked listeners by telling Frum that "women are only good for lying on their backs." Ballard later told writer Earl McRae that he couldn't "stand feminist broads. They're a bunch of frustrated old maids. A lot of them phoned me after the Frum incident and complained. I said to them. 'What's the matter, honey, can't get a man? You want my body?' Boy, they went nuts. I loved it."

- Referring to gentlemanly Inge Hammerstrom, a Swedish forward who joined the Leafs at the same time as Borje Salming, Ballard commented: "Hammerstrom could go in the corners with half a dozen eggs in his pocket and not break one of them."

- He called Czech defector Vaclav Nedomansky "a traitor" for fleeing his homeland in order to play hockey in Canada with the Toronto Toros of the WHA. Ironically, a few months later, when Ballard signed two Czech players, Peter Ihnacek and Miroslav Frycer, he called them "brave young men for having the guts to leave their native land to start life anew in Canada."

- He refused to converse with *Toronto Star* hockey writer Frank Orr because he disliked some of Orr's columns. Behind Orr's back he called the heterosexual sportswriter "a queer."

- He threatened to bar Bobby Hull from Maple Leaf Gardens because Hull was thinking of removing some of his mementos from the Hockey Hall of Fame. When Hull was hired to do appearances for *Hockey Night in Canada* out of Toronto and bluntly asked Ballard if the threat to keep him out of the Gardens was true, Ballard laughed and lied. "No way, Bobby. You're welcome in my rink anytime," he told the former scoring champ.

- During his early relationship with Leaf captain Darryl Sittler, he told reporters, "If I could have another son, I'd want one just like him." A few months later he was calling the popular Sittler a "cancer" on the team.

- When Gordie Howe scored his 1,000th career goal while playing in the WHA, Ballard refused to allow the news to be flashed on the scoreboard over center ice at the Gardens. "Why, that's not an accomplishment worthy or recognition," he scoffed. "A blind man can score goals in that league."

80

- When new private boxes were installed in Maple Leaf Gardens, Ballard had legendary broadcaster Foster Hewitt's famous broadcasting booth — the gondola — removed. It went to the incinerator instead of to the Hockey Hall of Fame. When there was a public outcry, Ballard said he would sell off Foster's favorite chair from the gondola and give the profits to charity. Then he acquired 25 chairs, painted Foster's name on the back of them, and sold them, as well. (In fact, Foster never did have one particular chair he used during his hundreds of Leaf broadcasts.)
- Ballard cut the salary of longtime scout Bob Davidson by two-thirds in order to force him to quit the Leaf organization. The ploy worked because Davidson promptly turned in his resignation.
- When two of his players, Sittler and Salming, signed up to take part in the popular TV intermission feature "Showdown," a series approved by the league, Ballard sought a court order to prevent the Leaf stars from participating. When his request was turned down, he banned the "Showdown" tapes from all Leaf telecasts, virtually throwing the segment's producers into bankruptcy.
- When the NHL ordered all teams to put players' names on the backs of their game jerseys, Ballard balked at the edict, fearing it would hurt the sale of game-day programs, which contained the lineups. When pressured by NHL president John Ziegler to

conform, Ballard had the players' names stitched on the jerseys — but in the same color as the jersey itself, making the names unrecognizable from any distance.

Clarence Campbell Goes to Jail

IN MARCH 1980 Clarence Campbell, former president of the National Hockey League, spent five hours in a Montreal jail cell. It was part of his sentence after he was convicted of wrongdoing in the Dorval Sky Shops scandal. Campbell was also fined $25,000.

The 74-year-old hockey Hall of Famer's stay in jail was "a symbolic sentence," according to Mr. Justice Melvin Rothman of the Quebec Superior Court. It was lenient because of the judge's consideration for Campbell's failing health.

The previous month Campbell and businessman Gordon Brown were found guilty of conspiring to give Senator Louis Giguere $95,000 in exchange for an extension on the lease of the duty-free Sky Shops at Dorval Airport. The sentence placed a shameful blemish on the reputation of the man who had preached integrity in hockey throughout his long career as NHL president.

The Youngest Referee

AGES OF EARLY-DAY hockey referees were seldom recorded, but since many arbiters were players recruited from other teams, their youth was taken for granted. Frank Patrick would certainly rank among the youngest of the players chosen to handle important matches. On nights when he wasn't starring for his own club in Montreal, this 18-year-old was often the referee in games played elsewhere. By age 20 he was selected to referee two important Stanley Cup series.

The Missing Officials

ON JANUARY 15, 1983, a blizzard swept through New England and prevented NHL referee Ron Fournier and linesman Dan Marouelli from getting to their next assignment — a game in Hartford between the Whalers and the New York Islanders. So linesman Ron Foyt, who did make it to the game on time, consulted the NHL rule book and found a solution to the problem. If he took over as referee, he was permitted to recruit a player from each club to serve as linesmen in the game. He had no trouble finding volunteers. Gary Howatt of the Islanders and Mickey Vulcan of the Whalers were both nursing minor injuries. But both could skate. And both were happy to assist Foyt because "it was a once-in-a-lifetime" opportunity.

So the game was played and the first period went by without a hitch. During the intermission, Fournier and Marouelli finally arrived and replaced the two players who had helped create an NHL "first." The two volunteers, Howatt and Vulcan, are the only two modern-day players ever to act as game officials in the NHL.

83

King Clancy Serves as a Goal Judge

THE LATE KING CLANCY was hockey's jack-of-all-trades. In his career he was a player, a coach, a referee, and an executive. And on at least two occasions he served as a goal judge during a game — a role he didn't particularly relish. Here is how he described his first stint as the official in charge of the red light.

"When I was with the Leafs in the thirties, I came down to Maple Leaf Gardens one day to watch a junior game between Niagara Falls and the Ottawa Primroses. Midway through the game, there was a problem with the goal judge. Whether the fellow got sick or fell off his stool and hurt himself, I don't recall. But they did ask me to fill in for him. I said, 'Sure, I'll help out. What's so hard about being a goal judge?'

"Remember, in those days, there was no protective cage to sit in. Nothin' like that. The goal judge sat right in with the crowd, more or less. I just got settled in my position when the Ottawa boys scored a goal. At least I thought they scored one because I snapped on the red light.

"I was amazed at what happened next. Some of the fans were jolted right out of their seats when they saw that little red light flash on. They began screaming at me, claiming that the puck didn't go into the net. A bunch of the Niagara Falls fans — a really tough-looking gang — began leaping over the seats, headed in my direction.

"I'll tell you. I cleared out of there in a hurry. The cops were called and it was a long time before I could resume my place. And during the rest of the

84

game, I kept sneaking looks over my shoulder to make sure I wasn't going to get attacked again.

"After that game, I vowed I'd never be a goal judge again, but I was persuaded to take the job on one other occasion. It was another big junior game at the Gardens, and I was handling the job well — that is, until I became the victim of a cruel practical joke.

During the play, the puck was lofted up against the side of the net just in front of me. The puck didn't even come close to going in the net, but suddenly the crowd was in an uproar. Fans were screaming at me and shaking their fists at me and I had no idea why they were so outraged. I hadn't flashed the red light. But *somebody* had, because when I looked up it was on.

"The referee skated up to me and asked, 'What's the matter with you, King? Why'd you turn the light on?'

Jack-of-all-trades King Clancy — he had a million and one stories.
(Hockey Hall of Fame)

85

"'I never touched the light,' I told him. 'Maybe there's an electrical problem.' I couldn't believe this was happening to me.

"That's when I glanced over and saw Charlie Conacher standing nearby. He was laughing his head off. Well, I knew right then how the red light got turned on. Charlie had sneaked up behind me, reached around, and flipped the light switch. Right then and there I decided to get out of the goal-judging business. It had too many surprises to suit me."

A Former Goon Controls the Game

NHL REFEREE PAUL STEWART comes by his whistle-tooting honestly. His grandfather, Bill Stewart, was a big league referee and a major league umpire before he took a job in the NHL as rookie coach of the Chicago Blackhawks.

Big Bill may have lacked coaching experience, but he knew enough about handling athletes to astonish all the so-called experts. Stewart took the Blackhawks all the way to the Stanley Cup championship in 1938. And he did it with a team that won only 14 games during the regular season.

Paul Stewart speaks with pride of his granddaddy's record. And if you ask, he'll show you the gold watch fob he inherited from his distinguished grandparent, a prized souvenir of that long-ago Cup victory.

As inheritor of the famous Stewart bloodlines, you might assume that Paul was a stickler for fair play growing up, a play-it-by-the-rules kind of guy in his own athletic endeavors. As a player, his ap-

86

proach was quite the opposite. His record as a goon and troublemaker in pro hockey, especially the World Hockey Association, is truly astonishing.

The native of Boston started his pro career in 1975 with the Binghampton Dusters in the North American Hockey League, where he quickly gained a reputation as a brawler. In his second season he punched a referee between periods of a game after being cut by a high stick. The offense drew an eight-game suspension. His pro career included a two-year stint in the WHA with the Cincinnati Stingers, and finally — a dream come true — 20 games with the Quebec Nordiques in the NHL. In five pro seasons he logged more than 1,200 penalty minutes.

He tried a normal job after retiring as a player but found he missed hockey. "I loved the action, the involvement, the travel," he says. "So I decided to make a comeback — this time as a referee."

Now 37, the popular arbiter explains his switch from pugilist to peacekeeper this way: "It's no different than a fellow who fought on one side during the war, then turns around and becomes an ally. I discovered years ago it's more fun to hand out penalties than to receive them — especially when I can earn more money refereeing than I ever did as a player."

Foster Hewitt's First Broadcast

FOSTER HEWITT, the dean of hockey play-by-play broadcasters, died of Alzheimer's disease in 1985. During the sixties, I shared space in the famous gondola at Maple Leaf Gardens with this broadcasting legend, and from time to time he would reminisce about some of the most memorable moments in his brilliant career.

One date he would never forget was March 22, 1923. On the morning of that day Basil Lake, the radio editor of the *Toronto Star,* gave Foster a unique assignment — to broadcast a hockey game that night between the Kitchener Seniors and Toronto Parkdale from Mutual Street Arena. Foster, then an 18-year-old cub reporter, accepted the assignment with a great deal of reluctance. He had been on the job since dawn that day and he was weary, there was a storm sweeping through Toronto and, most important, he had no idea how to broadcast a fast game like hockey.

But Lake insisted he do the job. Hadn't Foster expressed an interest in getting involved with this new medium of radio? Hadn't he dabbled in boxing and other sports? Then give it a try.

That night, fortified with a five-cent hot dog for nourishment, Foster helped set up the space required at rinkside. His booth was an airtight, glass-enclosed box — about the size of a broom closet. Fortunately he remembered to purchase a program listing the players' names and numbers, and when the puck was dropped, he began talking. Early in the broadcast he even introduced a phrase that would become internationally famous — "He shoots . . . he scores!" He told me once: "I didn't plan to use it. It just came out. And in time it seemed to catch the fancy of a lot of listeners."

The air in his booth soon became warm and stuffy. He began to perspire, and the glass surrounding his tiny cubicle misted over. He was so uncomfortable that he couldn't wait for the final whistle. But the game ended in a 3–3 tie and overtime was ordered.

88

Foster talked on through three 10-minute overtime periods before the action finally came to a halt. Had he been given a say in the matter he would have vowed then and there never to enter a broadcasting booth again under any circumstances.

However, the response from listeners to his first broadcast was astonishing, so overwhelming that more play-by-play broadcasts were scheduled and Foster was ordered to do them — whether he liked it or not.

Before his second game he wisely had some holes for ventilation drilled through the glass enclosing his booth. "I really didn't mind becoming Toronto's first play-by-play man," he told me. "I just didn't want to be the first to suffocate on the job."

Foster Wasn't the First

ASK A MILLION HOCKEY FANS who broadcast the first hockey game and they will tell you it was Foster Hewitt. On march 22, 1923, Hewitt handled the play-by-play of a senior game from Mutual Street Arena in Toronto between the Parkdale team and Kitchener.

But was he shinny's first commentator? Not according to the *Regina Leader-Post.* Reporter Ron Campbell, writing in that newspaper in 1972, reveals that Pete Parker, a hockey fan turned broadcaster, called the play-by-play of the Western Canada Hockey League playoffs between Edmonton and Regina on CKCK radio on the night of march 14, 1923 — nine days before Foster's historic broadcast in Toronto.

A special closed-in cubicle was built to house

89

Parker and his equipment. The front of his booth was covered with a huge sheet of celluloid, which Parker lifted with one hand when he thought crowd noises would enhance his delivery.

Parker, in relating the story of the first hockey broadcast to the *Leader-Post,* recalled that "the players didn't wear numbers on their sweaters, but that represented no problem because I was familiar with all of the boys and knew them all by sight."

Dick Irvin, Senior, who went on to a great coaching career in the NHL with Toronto, Montreal, and Chicago, played for Regina in that game. Duke Keats was the star forward for Edmonton. Keats set up the winning goal by Art Gagne in a 1–0 Edmonton victory. Two nights later, back in Edmonton, Keats scored the series-winning goal in overtime.

Parker's broadcast of the first playoff game brought dozens of letters from listeners throughout southern Saskatchewan and from many U.S. centers, as well. The next season he was hired to broadcast all of the home games of the Regina Caps on CKCK.

Parker's friends and fellow broadcasters always resented the fact that Foster Hewitt received the credit for being the game's first play-by-play man.

Well, Excuse Me!

WHEN PUNCH IMLACH was hired (for the second time) as general manager of the Toronto Maple Leafs in the seventies, he antagonized players and fans with his "let's clean house" approach. He dumped players he felt were still loyal to former general manager Jim Gregory. He traded players like Pat Boutette, Dave Hutchi-

90

son, Tiger Williams, and others. And he infuriated everybody when he swapped popular Lanny McDonald, a genuine Leaf hero, to Colorado. And he caused another ripple of anger to sweep through Toronto when he suggested he would get rid of captain Darryl Sittler, too, if Sittler didn't have a bothersome no-trade clause in his contract.

Meanwhile Imlach had hired Joe Crozier, an old friend, to coach the Leafs. When team owner Harold Ballard, never one to hide his emotions, expressed his disdain for Crozier, the players saw their opportunity to get back at Imlach. They simply didn't listen to or perform for Crozier. Their attitude infuriated the coach and general manager.

Crozier, sensing he was about to be fired by Ballard, called a team meeting and lectured the Leafs for their behavior. When he finished, there was silence in the Leaf dressing room. It was left up to free spirit Ian Turnbull to come up with an appropriate response. He lifted one leg and cut loose with a thunderous fart. That about said it all.

George "Punch" Imlach, the Maple Leafs' tough-as-nails coach and general manager.

91

When You Hear the Whistle, Pass the Puck!

IN 1926, WHEN THE CHICAGO BLACKHAWKS joined the National Hockey League, Major Frederic McLaughlin, the eccentric team owner, hired Pete Muldoon as the first of many Chicago coaches. Muldoon will be remembered for his Don Cherry-like shirt collars and little else, and when he was fired months later, it was said he placed a curse on the Blackhawks, a hex that kept them from a first-place finish in the NHL until 1961. Actually there was no curse. The story was concocted by an inventive sportswriter Jim Coleman after wrestling with a rum bottle most of the night.

Of the dozen or so coaches who followed Muldoon, a man named Godfrey Matheson brought the strangest theories to hockey. Matheson's main claim to fame was the fact that he had guided a team of Winnipeg kids to a midget league championship. When McLaughlin heard about this monumental accomplishment, he hired Matheson on the spot.

Matheson soon introduced some ultramodern coaching ideas that left his players, the fans, and ultimately the team owner in a state of bewilderment, if not shock. His most notable innovation was the whistle system of coaching. From behind the bench Matheson would signal plays by blowing a whistle. One blast was a signal for the puck carrier to pass the puck, two blasts called for a shot on goal, three toots on the whistle meant the Hawks were to tighten up defensively, and so on. Matheson's system may rank as the goofiest coaching strategy ever conceived. The players found it

92

impossible to count or keep track of the whistles. Some shot when they should have passed, others passed when they should have shot, and a few ignored the whistle-tooter altogether. One can only imagine how the referees reacted to all those piercing whistles from the bench.

Before Matheson could come up with any more bright ideas to revolutionize coaching, owner McLaughlin sent him packing. But it wasn't long before he made another oddball coaching choice. He hired Bill Stewart, a baseball umpire and hockey referee, to guide the Hawks. And this time he got lucky, for Stewart took the Blackhawks all the way to the Stanley Cup in 1938.

Coaches Do the Silliest Things

ROGER NEILSON, when he coached the Buffalo Sabres, once threw sticks and a water bottle onto the ice because he didn't care much for the officiating in a game one night.

Tom Webster, coach of the L.A. Kings, hurled a hockey stick, javelin-style, at a referee during an NHL game, hitting the official on the foot.

Billy Reay, when he coached Buffalo in the American Hockey League, once got into a fistfight with the team's announcer.

Murph Chamberlain, another Buffalo coach, once threw a bucket of pucks onto the ice while a game was in progress.

Jacques Demers and Mike Keenan are two NHL coaches who have been accused of tossing pennies onto the ice to create a time-out during games.

Toe Blake of the Montreal Canadiens once

93

stormed across the ice and punched a referee. He was subsequently fined $2,000.

A coach of a junior team in western Canada once stripped to the waist during a game. Nobody knows why.

Toronto's Punch Imlach once put his skates on at the Leaf bench, opened the gate, and was about to skate out and argue a point with the referee when he had second thoughts and retreated.

Emile Francis of the Rangers once scooted around the rink to tell a goal judge off. Fans intervened, Francis found himself in the middle of a battle, and his players had to climb over the high glass, leap into the throng, and rescue him.

Jack Adams of Detroit, with his team leading Toronto 3–1 in games, jumped onto the ice at the end of game four of the 1941 Stanley Cup finals and started punching referee Mel Harwood. It marked a turning point in the series. Adams was suspended indefinitely, his team sagged, and Toronto won three in a row and captured the Stanley Cup in what has been called "hockey's greatest comeback."

When Goal Judges Were Stripped of Their Power

IN HOCKEY'S CRADLE DAYS the goal judges — often men selected at random and pulled from the stands just before game time — were compelled to make the final decision when a goal was scored. If they erred, or were thought to have erred, the fans howled their displeasure. The referee, if he felt so inclined, had the authority to send one or

94

both judges back to their seats and call on a couple of volunteers to replace them. It was a bizarre system by today's standards, but perfectly acceptable to turn-of-the-century hockey fans.

Later the power of awarding a goal was stripped from the goal judges and awarded to the referee, and it is easy to single out the reason for the change. Goal judges were most often residents of the community in which the game was played. Therefore it was assumed that their decisions, more often than not, favored the home team. Referees, on the other hand, were often "outsiders," imported from another community some distance away and therefore (it was fervently hoped) they were unlikely to hold any bias toward one team or the other. It was also thought that the referee might have a better vantage point to see whether or not a goal was actually scored.

One game, played in Morrisburg, Ontario, shortly after the turn of the century, may have precipitated the change. While hosting archrival Cornwall, one of the Morrisburg players skated down the ice and apparently scored. The goal judge, a Morrisburg native, waved his little flag, signaling a goal. The Cornwall players protested, claiming the puck didn't enter the net. When their complaints were shrugged off, the players and their fans drew up an affidavit bearing the names of 200 spectators who swore the goal hadn't been scored. One of their number, a Cornwall lawyer, presented the affidavit to league officials. It was an impressive-looking document.

When the Morrisburg fans got wind of this initiative, they were quick to respond. They, too, scurried around seeking witnesses, and overnight they collected the names of 200 witnesses who swore they saw the puck enter the net.

The Cornwall supporters never did get the original ruling overturned, but the pressure they exerted did force a change in league policy. Shortly afterward league officials declared that the referee would have the final say whenever a goal was scored.

The Team That Never Should Have Won the Cup

TAKE THE CHICAGO BLACKHAWKS — please! That was what Chicago fans were saying in 1938 when the Hawks stumbled their way to a mere 14 wins in a 48-game schedule. The Hawks scored only 97 goals all season, less than two per game, the puniest goal production of the eight NHL clubs.

"No wonder they're a lousy team," some fans grumbled. "The club is coached by a former baseball umpire and a referee. What does he know about running a hockey team?"

They were referring to 43-year-old Bill Stewart, who indeed spent his summers umpiring big league ball games and his previous winter as chief of NHL referees. But Hawks owner Major Frederic McLaughlin took a fancy to Stewart's fiery umpiring style and figured he could inject some of that same spirit into his hockey team. So he awarded Stewart a two-year coaching contract.

Even though Chicago squeaked into the playoffs in 1938, they were given virtually no chance of advancing to the finals. One Hawk defenseman,

Roger Jenkins, even bet goalie Mike Karakas a wheelbarrow ride through Chicago that the Hawks wouldn't win the Stanley Cup.

Predictably the Hawks lost the first game of their two-out-of-three first-round series with the Montreal Canadiens. Then Karakas caught fire and the Hawks won two straight games, eliminating the surprised Habs.

In their next series versus the New York Americans, the Hawks again fell behind, losing game one. But once more they fought back to win two in a row, leaving the Amerks shaking their heads in disbelief. Suddenly the team that was scorned and humiliated all season found itself in the Stanley Cup finals, facing the powerful Toronto Maple Leafs and their ace goaltender Turk Broda.

Prior to game one the Hawks were plunged into dire straits when goalie Mike Karakas couldn't fit his skate on over a broken toe suffered in the previous series against New York. When Toronto owner Conn Smythe turned down Stewart's request to use a capable substitute, a frantic last-minute search was conducted for little-known netminder Alfie Moore, a Leaf castoff who was found nursing a few beers in a Toronto tavern.

"Don't worry, Bill," Moore said when he was led into the Chicago dressing room. "I haven't been on skates for a couple of weeks, but I'll make those bastards eat the puck."

He did. He made 26 saves, most of them brilliant. One save was a real laugher. The puck hit him in the seat of the pants, and he spun around to see if it was in the net. The Hawks went on to win the game 3–1, and Moore thumbed his nose at the Leaf bench as he left the ice.

Smythe, mad as hell at Moore, banned him from any further competition, and the Hawks, for game two, were forced to employ Paul Goodman, a 28-year-old minor leaguer with no NHL experience. The Leafs not only beat Goodman (who hadn't been on skates in three weeks) by a 5–1 score, but they laid out several Hawks during the contest with crushing checks and flailing fists.

Coach Stewart told the press that he had to visit the hospital before game three to look in on a half-dozen of his boys. "They were laid out with cuts and bruises, and my star center, Doc Romnes, had a broken nose," he complained.

Romnes was wearing a Purdue University football helmet to protect his nose when he took to the ice at the Chicago Stadium before 18,496 fans two nights later. It was the largest crowd in NHL history. Luckily coach Stewart had Karakas back by then. The injured goalie was able to squeeze his broken toe into his skate boot and went on to play an outstanding game. Doc Romnes scored the winner late in the third period, and Chicago took a 2–1 lead in the series.

Karakas and Turk Broda provided most of the thrills in game four, stopping shot after shot. Late in the second period, with the score tied 1–1, the Hawks' Carl Voss stole the puck and beat Broda to give Chicago a 2–1 lead. Then came one of the most incredible goals in playoff history. Jack Shill of the Hawks, hoping to kill some time on the clock, lofted a shot toward Broda — from 150 feet away. Broda moved out and dropped to his knees to trap the puck, but it skipped past him and into the open net. Chicago led 3–1.

The Leafs pulled out all the stops in the third

98

period, but the strategy backfired when Mush March broke away to make it 4–1. With time running out Stewart instructed Johnny Gottselig, a marvelous stickhandler, to "rag the puck," and that was just what he did, stickhandling around and through the Toronto players as if they were pylons.

When it was over, the team that didn't have a chance threw their coach up onto their shoulders, almost dropping him in the process, and Karakas reminded Jenkins to show up for the wheelbarrow ride. In the weeks that followed, Bill Stewart, the umpire who won the Stanley Cup, was the toast of Chicago. But the backslapping he happily endured soon stopped. The team owner, Major McLaughlin, fired him the following season.

PART

LORE AND LEGENDS

Was Hockey Invented by the British Royal Family?

IN MY RESEARCH into hockey's beginnings recently I came across an article written in 1937 by Ian Gordon, a British journalist who claims that hockey owes its life to the British Royal Family. In his astonishing claim Gordon writes:

> While it is true that the Dominion across the Atlantic [Canada] has nursed and developed ice hockey to the fine pitch of physical perfection and precision that has earned it the title of the fastest game on earth, the idea originated at Windsor Castle.

> The game is in modern times labelled "the national sport of Canada" but it owes its life to the Royal Family. Among its first players are included two King Emperors, and the first excited spectators were ladies of the Royal Household.

> In the hard winter of 1853 the house party at the country palace looked for diversion on the frozen lake on the grounds. The idea was born to play a game of field hockey on the ice; sides were chosen, sticks found, and the bung from a barrel acquired to take the place of the ball, which bounced too much for any accurate control.

> While Queen Victoria and her attendants stood by giving encouragement, officers of the guards skated over the surface trying to score into the net defended by the Prince Consort. The result was not recorded but history tells that the players were rewarded with a well-spiced rum punch.

103

It was more than 20 years later that the game crossed the ocean to Canada. On a visit to England, a student of McGill University came upon a game of field hockey. His versatile brain followed along the same lines as those pioneers at Windsor Castle, and on his return to his studies that winter he called together a band of enthusiasts, pointed out the natural playing resources of the severe Canadian winter, with its months of ice and snow, and promptly organized the first team at McGill University.

Support later came from an unexpected source; not a Canadian sportsman but from an Englishman. Lord Stanley, the Governor General, presented a handsome trophy, and from that time the success and ever-growing interest in the sport in Canada was assured.

Of course, Maritime historians such as Howard Dill and Dr. Garth Vaughn claim that some form of hockey had been played in Nova Scotia, notably on Windsor's Long Pond, in the early 1800s, or almost a half century before the games described above at Windsor Castle.

Bizarre Olympic Victory for Great Britain

IN THE EARLY THIRTIES Bunny Ahearne was becoming a person to be reckoned with in international hockey. And it was Ahearne who was responsible for putting the first blight on Canada's unblemished hockey record at the Olympics in 1936.

104

Months prior to the Olympic Games the wily entrepreneur compiled a list of all amateur players in Canada who had been born in the British Isles. Most had immigrated to Canada as young children and over the years had mastered most of hockey's skills in Canadian rinks. The best of these amateurs were lured to London by Ahearne, who found a league for them to play in and slipped them as much as $50 a week to cover expenses. One of the most talented was goaltender Jimmy Foster.

Ahearne recruited yet another Canadian, Percy Nicklin, to coach a team in his house league, and when the Winter Olympics of 1936 were staged in Garmisch, Germany, Ahearne assembled a "British" entry composed of the London-based imports with the experienced Nicklin at the helm.

The Canadian representatives that year were from Port Arthur — the Bearcats, a team of little distinction and one that had to be bolstered by five good players from the Montreal area before leaving Canada. The Bearcats ran into a stone wall when they faced Jimmy Foster and the British entry in what they were led to believe was a semifinal match. Foster played the game of his life and yielded just one goal while his mates managed two. It was the first defeat ever for Canada in Olympic hockey competition. Despite the loss, the Canadian players weren't talking about revenge. Ahead lay the final round of the tournament, and they looked forward to getting another crack at Foster.

Then came an astonishing statement from Ahearne. He insisted that a final-round match was out of the question. It was unnecessary, since Canada had already lost once to his British team. Furious, Canadian officials entered a strong protest, and an emergency meeting was called at which a smiling Ahearne said, "Fine, let's vote on it." To Canada's disgust five nations sided with Ahearne, a man once described by a journalist as "capable of acting unscrupulously to gain his own advantage." Only Germany felt the Canadian team was being cheated of their rightful chance at the title.

Ahearne smirked as Britain was awarded the gold medal, even though the British had played one less game than Canada and had fewer tournament wins. Canada's records was 7–1, Britain's 5–2.

Bizarre? You bet.

For the next four decades Ahearne was a sharp thorn in the hide of Canadian hockey. Jim Coleman, one of Canada's most highly respected hockey writers, in his book *Hockey Is Our Game,* called Ahearne "a Machiavellian strategist" and "a double-dealing, self-serving little rascal from the opening face-off to the final buzzer."

Despite his wily ways and the antipathy he often showed toward Canadians, Ahearne was honored by the Hockey Hall of Fame in 1977. His induction surprised many, including Jim Coleman, who wrote: "Nothing he did in his old age appeared to qualify him for the honor of enshrinement in the Hockey Hall of Fame, that is, primarily, a Canadian institution."

Bruins' Leading Scorer Suspended for Life

IT HAPPENED ALMOST half a century ago — in 1948. Hockey star Don Gallinger suddenly found himself banished from the game he loved.

Gallinger, a versatile athlete who turned down

106

pro baseball offers from the Philadelphia Athletics and the Boston Red Sox, was summoned to the NHL at the age of 17. The shifty centerman was Boston's leading scorer when his career suddenly skidded to a halt at age 22. In the final month of the 1947–48 season, NHL president Clarence Campbell suspended Gallinger for life for gambling on hockey games.

"It was such a dreadful thing," Gallinger told *Toronto Sun* reporter Steve Simmons in 1989. "Nobody knows more about depression and despair than I do. I was just 22. I would never wish on people what I have gone through.

"Sure I bet on games. But I never fixed a game. When they called me in, I wasn't worried. I never thought they could pin anything on me."

But they did. Gallinger and Billy Taylor, then with the Rangers, were identified as having done business with a Detroit bookmaker and racketeer named James Tamer. Police taps on the former prison inmate's phone calls produced information about hockey bets, and the names Taylor and Gallinger surfaced.

The final bet Gallinger made was a $1,000 wager on a game between the Bruins and the Blackhawks. The Bruins won the game and Gallinger figured in the tying goal. He lost the bet.

At first, when called upon to explain his actions, Gallinger denied everything. He knew the charges against him would be difficult to prove. Only if Taylor confessed to any wrongdoing would Gallinger be implicated. Taylor decided to confess and was suspended for life.

A few months later, in a five-hour meeting with Campbell, Gallinger finally admitted his guilt. He, too, drew a lifetime suspension. Gallinger never forgave the league president for acting as judge and jury, and it always puzzled him why Babe Pratt, a third player who had confessed to gambling on hockey games two years earlier, had drawn a mere 16-game suspension. Incredibly neither Gallinger nor Taylor was represented by a lawyer, and some of the evidence — the wiretaps obtained by Detroit police — were obtained illegally.

All hockey avenues were closed to the banished stars. Gallinger applied for coaching and management positions with several teams but was shunned wherever he applied. He lost his 11-year-old daughter to cancer. His wife left him, taking two other children with her. The business he was in collapsed. "I was lost and afraid," he told Simmons. "I was ready to blow my brains out."

Some say it was an act of mercy when Campbell reinstated Gallinger and Taylor in 1970. Others say the NHL president feared a lawsuit from the banished pair. Taylor made a successful return to the fold, securing scouting jobs. But Gallinger's attempts to find hockey employment in the league that banished him met with failure at every turn.

Did Hockey Begin on Howard Dill's Pumpkin Farm?

IN THE *BOSTON GLOBE* of October 3, 1991, on the first page of the sports section, there is a color photo of Howard Dill, arms folded, sitting on a giant pumpkin. From under his peaked cap he gazes out over a small pond on his 250-acre farm

108

near Windsor, Nova Scotia. The murky patch of water that attracts his wistful stare is known as Long Pond or Steel Pond. The caption under the photo reads: "Howard Dill dreams of days when hockey, in possibly its earliest form, was played on the pond that sits on his property."

Writer Kevin Dupont of the *Globe* came all the way from Boston to see the pond and to interview Dill, a four-time world champion pumpkin grower, a hockey historian, and an assembler of a marvelous collection of hockey memorabilia. Although arguments abound as to when and where the game of hockey originated, Howard Dill, and the good people of Windsor, believe the nondescript patch of water on the Dill property should be recognized as hockey's birthplace.

Was hockey born on this pond in Windsor, Nova Scotia? Pumpkin king Howard Dill certainly thinks so.

To back his claim that his pond is historically significant, Dill points to an 1844 story in the London periodical *Attaché,* in which author Thomas Haliburton writes about hurley, a game closely resembling hockey, being played on Long Pond circa 1810. Haliburton recounts his boyhood school days at King's College, today known as King's Edgehill School, which stands a short distance from the small pond in question. Haliburton's words are possibly the oldest written evidence of hockey being played in Canada: ". . . and the boys let out racin', yellin', hollerin' and whoopin' like mad with pleasure . . . and the game at bass [*sic*] in the field, or hurley on the long pond on the ice . . ."

"The way I see it," Dill says, "the proof is right there in that story." The man who knows pumpkins (he grows 600-pounders and sells the seeds all over the world, advising clients to "plant 'em and jump back fast") also knows his hockey history.

As for the pond, in its heyday in the thirties and forties, kids played hockey on it all the time. School kids mingled with town kids. They would skate and play hockey on the pond all day. At night they would light bonfires and toast marshmallows. They had been doing it for generations. Why wouldn't they be doing it as far back as 1800?

Forty or fifty years ago, when Dill played hockey on the pond, it was close to 200 feet long and about 50 feet wide. Over the years the water level has dropped and now the pond is a third of its former size. Dill thinks the pond should be recognized as the cradle of hockey in North America — until someone steps forward with conclusive written proof that it isn't. "It should be preserved," Dill

110

says. "Maybe a sign erected so people who come here can look at it and say, 'That's where hockey began, back in the early 1800s.'"

When Royalty Played Hockey

JOURNALIST IAN GORDON, writing about hockey in England, reveals that Lord Stanley, donor of the family trophy, actually played the game — at least on one occasion. And among his companions were the most famous bluebloods in the British Empire:

The [hockey] team spirit in England was encouraged in the 1890s in a very unexpected way. A Royal team was formed at Buckingham Palace in the winter of 1895, and when a hard frost — which gave sufficient ice on the lake behind the Palace — rewarded earnest desire, a challenge was issued to a team skippered by Lord Stanley, the Earl of Derby. Buckingham Palace included in their line-up the Prince of Wales, later to become King Edward VII, and the Duke of York, who afterwards became King George V.

The rival teams were six a side. Lord Stanley had four members of his family playing alongside him, and their Canadian experience gave them a big advantage. This resulted in numerous goals being chalked up to their credit, while the Palace combination could only score once.

Until the end of the century, hockey came in for considerable patronage from the Royal Family,

111

and at most club games there was at least one supporter from Buckingham Palace to follow the play closely.

Hengler's Rink in London — now the Royal Palladium — was the favourite place, and many members of the European Royal Families, when visiting London, were escorted there to be initiated into the daring game.

Although England has thus played such a big part in giving a historical background to ice hockey, the sport had little public favour here. The main reason for this was the lack of opportunities for training boys to skate. Hard winters failed to materialize as they did in the "good old days" and the post-war youngster knew little of the joy of skimming over ice on two thin blades of steel.

The Goalie Wore Boxing Gloves

AUTHOR GEORGE TATOMYR'S BOOK *Beyond the Uke Line* profiles each of 55 hockey players of Ukrainian descent who played in the NHL. One of the most famous was Bronco Horvath, who centered Johnny Bucyk and Vic Stasiuk on the potent Uke Line for the Boston Bruins over 30 years ago. Others who excelled in the NHL were goalies Terry Sawchuk, Johnny Bower, and Turk Broda, and forwards Mike Bossy, Dale Hawerchuk, Bernie Federko, Stan Smyl, Dennis Maruk, Tom Lysiak, Bill Mosienko, and yes,

112

even Eddie "Clear the Track" Shack. Over the years Ukrainians have accounted for close to 8,000 NHL goals.

Tatomyr's research indicates that hockey's start in the Ukraine had shaky beginnings. In the 1930s a team called the Lions competed in a Polish league. The Ukrainian goalie protected his head with a primitive face mask made out of a World War I army helmet. Sturdy metal bars attached to the helmet deflected pucks aimed at his face.

Hockey, like most sports, disappeared from the Ukraine during the war, but it surfaced again in the late forties. This time the players really had to improvise when it came to equipment. For example, the goalie on one team wore boxing gloves. Pieces of quilting protected shins and shoulders and were held in place by long underwear worn over top. During one postwar season, the Lions had only six gloves between them, and players were obliged to take turns wearing them.

They became accustomed to derisive laughter wherever they appeared. In their debut against a German team at Garmisch, their opponents laughed heartily at their ridiculous appearance. But the ill-equipped visitors laughed last by trouncing their hosts 18–4.

Forward Passing Opened Up the Game

PRIOR TO THE 1929–30 NHL season the league removed the shackles from the forward pass. Prior to that a player couldn't

113

pass forward to a teammate in the attacking zone. What is more, a team was no longer permitted to keep more than three players (including the goalie) in the defensive zone while the play was up the ice. Laggards who didn't move up with the play could receive a minor penalty. Did the new rules lead to more scoring? You bet they did.

In the 1928–29 season, before the new rules were initiated, the trend toward defensive hockey was so great that little George Hainsworth, the Montreal goalie, recorded 22 shutouts in 44 games and yielded only 43 goals to opposing shooters. Boston, the highest-scoring team in hockey, managed only 89 goals all season, and Toronto's Ace Bailey won the NHL scoring championship with a mere 22 goals and 10 assists for 32 points.

Compare those statistics with the following season when the new forward pass rule was in place. Every team in the NHL topped 100 goals, the Bruins leading the way with 179 — 90 more than they had scored the previous year. Cooney Weiland of Boston went on a scoring spree that netted him the Art Ross Trophy with 43 goals and 73 points. The previous year he had scored 11 goals and 18 points. Two other players, Dit Clapper of the Bruins and Howie Morenz of Montreal, hit the 40-goal plateau. Clapper had scored nine goals one year earlier, while Morenz netted 17.

Defensively Tiny Thompson, the Bruin netminder, was the only goalie to give up fewer than 100 goals. He yielded 98 (55 more than Hainsworth had given up the previous season) in winning the Vezina Trophy.

There is no doubt that the introduction of the

forward pass within all three zones on the ice contributed greatly to a huge increase in scoring in the NHL.

Al Hill Makes Sensational Debut

IT IS STILL THERE in the NHL record book — Al Hill's impressive rookie scoring mark. In his first big league game, on February 14, 1977, Hill was called up from Springfield of the American Hockey League to play in his first NHL game with the Philadelphia Flyers. The six-foot-one left winger responded with two goals and three assists against the St. Louis Blues for a five-point night. The Flyers won the game 6–4 and Hill won the hearts of Flyer fans. They figured — after a debut like that — he would soon become a Flyer immortal, right up there with Bobby Clarke and Bill Barber. Hill scored 36 seconds into the nationally televised game and went on to make the game a miserable experience for Blues goalie Yves Belanger.

But Hill's moment in the spotlight was brief. Never again would he come even close to matching the magic of his big league debut. After a handful of games, he was returned to Springfield and had to wait two more years before getting a chance to score NHL goal number three.

Hill played parts of the next four seasons with Philadelphia, spent the following four years in the minors, and was recalled by the Flyers for a handful of games in 1986–87 and 1987–88. In 221 NHL games he collected 40 goals. But his first two — plus three

115

assists — in his major league debut have kept his name in the record book since 1977.

Toronto Granites Wallop World's Best Amateurs at Chamonix

IN 1924 THE TORONTO GRANITES represented Canada at the Winter Olympic Games held in Chamonix, France. Old-timers say the Granites were absolutely the best amateur team ever to wear Canadian colors at the international level. The scores they compiled were truly extraordinary and will never be matched.

The Olympic ice surface in Chamonix was an open-air rink with boards measuring a scant 12 inches high. Spectators often tumbled into one another as they leaped to avoid flying pucks.

In the opening round the Granites walloped Czechoslovakia 30–0, then Sweden 22–0, and finally Switzerland 33–0. In a semifinal match the Granites humbled Great Britain 19–2, and in the final game with the United States the Canadians skated to an easy 6–1 triumph.

In five games played the Granites scored 110 goals and gave up a mere three. Top scorer in the tournament was Harry Watson, who collected 38 goals, an average of more than seven per game.

At one point early in the tournament Granite star defenseman Dunc Munro looked over his shoulder to find the Canadian net empty. Goaltender Jack Cameron, bored with so little work, had skated over to the side boards and was en-

116

gaged in a lively conversation with two attractive young ladies.

Leaders in the Futility League

THE 1928–29 CHICAGO BLACKHAWKS were arguably the most inept NHL team ever. That season the Hawks stumbled their way through eight straight games without scoring a single goal. They were shut out 21 times in the 44-game schedule and managed to score only 33 goals for the season. Vic Ripley was their leading scorer with 11 goals and two assists for 13 points.

But were the 1928–29 Hawks any worse than the Washington Capitals, a seventies expansion team? The Caps barely survived 1974–75, their initial NHL season. During an 80-game season, Washington shattered a modern-day record for futility with a mark of eight wins, 67 losses, and five ties. The Caps didn't merely lose games that season; they were humiliated in almost every outing. Twice they lost by 12–1 scores. They lost other games by 11–1 and 10–0. In one 11-game stretch they were shut out five times. By the end of the season they had given up 446 goals while scoring only 181. Along the way they established one NHL record for consecutive losses with 17 and another for consecutive losses on the road — 37. The team went through three coaches — Jim Anderson, who lasted 54 games (4–45–5), Red Sullivan (2–17), and Milt Schmidt (2–5). In the

1992–93 season the Caps did find some relief from their ignominy. The new Ottawa Senators franchise lost 38 consecutive games on the road to break the Caps' record.

One of the Washington forwards was 19-year-old Mike Marson, a black player who wasn't close to being ready for the rough grind of the NHL. Marson was the only player not to wear underwear under his white hockey pants. Under the bright lights, and when Marson started to sweat, it looked as if he wasn't wearing any pants at all. The fans thought it was pretty funny, and after a while the players were given new blue pants and used the white ones only in practice.

Two games stand out in the memory of Tommy Williams, who led the team in scoring and consoled his mates with words like "We've got a good team, fellows. We're just in the wrong league." The Caps finally snapped their 37-game road losing streak with a victory over the California Seals in Oakland in late March 1975. Recently, reflecting on that game with *Washington Times* sportswriter David Elfin, Williams said, "We grabbed an old trash can and painted it with a magic marker. Then, half dressed, we paraded that trash can over our heads and skated around the Oakland Arena. You'd think we'd just won the Stanley Cup.

"And in our final home game of the season," Williams adds, "we beat Pittsburgh 8–4, and Stan Gilbertson, who later lost a leg in an auto accident, scored three goals in three minutes and 26 seconds, a record for an American-born player. An old goat like me [Williams was 34] set a club record in that game with six points. After the game, the fans came out on the ice and we posed for photos with them

118

and signed autographs. It was a nice ending to a very long season."

Unpredictable Ice Conditions

IN MANY EARLY-DAY Stanley Cup matches spring weather made for atrocious ice conditions. Sometimes there would be bits of grass and mud showing, and pools of water on the ice were quite common. In one playoff game the puck fell through a hole in the ice and couldn't be recovered. In Toronto one spring there was so little ice covering the floor that players were said to be "running back and forth on the board floor." After another playoff game, a reporter wrote: "Thanks to the good work of the lifesavers, all the players were saved from drowning."

Occasionally too much ice would be a problem. In Edmonton in 1909 the ice was measured and found to be 18 inches thick. A man in Calgary who had invented a machine that shaved ice was hired. He came to Edmonton and used his amazing machine to shave several inches of surface ice away, creating ideal conditions for a forthcoming playoff game.

The Unlikely Hockey Hero

HE PLAYS A MAJOR ROLE in every game, but he can't skate, has never scored a goal, doesn't know the rules, and doesn't care who wins or loses. Hockey players say they admire the way he works his way around the ice, and they

119

scatter in all directions when they see him coming. He is, if you haven't already guessed, the world-famous Zamboni, the incredible ice-resurfacing machine, a rugged, reliable performer in arenas around the world since the forties.

The Zamboni, a household name wherever hockey is played, is the invention of the late Frank Zamboni of Paramount, California. Zamboni's odd-looking machine revolutionized hockey and made the game easier to play and more pleasurable to watch for millions of players and fans.

Zamboni, a native of Utah, moved to California as a young man to work in his brother's garage. Later he and his brother set up an ice-making plant, which turned out 50 tons of ice per day. Then, when millions of electric refrigerators killed the ice-making business, the brothers decided to erect a skating rink, using the old plant to make the artificial ice that covered the floor. But when the arena opened, the Zambonis found that resurfacing the ice became a problem. It required a lot of time and manpower.

In 1942 Frank Zamboni began to experiment with vehicles to do the job, and the first machine he built was pulled on a sled towed by a tractor. However, this primitive model didn't produce a smooth surface because it didn't pick up the snow adequately. In 1947 Zamboni tried again but without much more success. By 1949 he had a machine that gave good results. It would consistently create a good sheet of ice.

One day his strange machine caught the eye of the famous figure skater Sonja Henie, who was practicing at the Zamboni rink for her ice show. Henie ordered a second machine and used it on her nationwide tour. Wherever she appeared rink oper-

120

ators made inquiries, and soon Frank Zamboni was getting phone calls and letters from all over North America. Since those early days, his unique ice machines have been in demand from rink operators in dozens of countries around the globe.

For a time his machine was known simply as "the ice resurfacer." Then one night at a hockey game some leather-lunged fan yelled out: "Get the damn Zamboni out and make some new ice!" The man didn't know it at the time, but he gave hockey a new name.

Moosomin First in Saskatchewan Hockey

THE PROVINCE OF SASKATCHEWAN was formed in 1905, but hockey was a fixture there long before that. Even so, it took a strange set of circumstances to bring the winter sport to that region of Canada.

It seems that a man involved with hockey equipment in Toronto received an order from Winnipeg one day. The request was for a couple of dozen hockey sticks, which were in short supply in the Manitoba capital. Somewhere en route west the address tag attached to the bundle was lost and the precious sticks never reached their destination. In time they surfaced in Birtle, Manitoba, where they were placed in a storage room by the station agent.

A traveling salesman stopped by one day to visit the agent, and the conversation turned to hockey. The agent showed the salesman the hockey sticks and said he had been having a lot of trouble locating the owner. Somehow a deal was made. The salesman,

121

a resident of Moosomin, Saskatchewan, and obviously a smooth talker, left with the sticks.

Returning to Moosomin, the salesman recruited some neighbors and distributed the sticks. A patch of nearby ice was cleared of snow and the first hockey game in that part of Saskatchewan was played — on a January day in 1895.

It was, of course, a makeshift game at best, with the players using a lacrosse ball for a puck. The participants were forced to play heads-up hockey right from the start, mainly because of a well casing in the center of the ice from which they drew water to flood the ice.

Smitty Made *The Guinness Book of Records*

IN THE HOCKEY RECORD BOOKS Toronto-born Normie Smith is listed as the winning goalie in the opening game of the semifinal round of the 1936 NHL playoffs. He starred in the longest game of hockey ever played.

On March 24, 1936, the Detroit Red Wings faced off against the Montreal Maroons at the Montreal Forum. Who could have known the teams were about to set an endurance record that would last for over a half century and maybe forever?

There was no scoring through sixty minutes of regulation time, and the teams moved into overtime. Period after period of overtime play was played, taking the game into the wee hours of the morning. Finally, in the sixth overtime period, after 116 minutes and 30 seconds of extra time, Detroit's Mud Bruneteau, a two-goal scorer during the regu-

122

lar season, slipped the puck past Lorne Chabot in the Montreal goal. The winner came at 2:25 a.m.

"The *Guinness* people did some research into that game and figured I'd set a world record with 92 saves in hockey's longest shutout," Smith said from his retirement home in Florida in 1987. "I remember the ice was very soft that night and my pads were soaking wet from the water on the ice. My underwear was soaked right through. We were all totally exhausted at the end.

"Between periods the coach gave us a little brandy to drink — just a sip or two — to give us energy and keep us going. A lot of the fans left when the game passed midnight. They had to get up early in the morning."

What is often overlooked is that Smith shut out the Maroons again two nights later, and it wasn't until game three of the series, when Montreal's Gus Marker finally scored on Smith at 12:02 of the first period, that the Detroit netminder's remarkable shutout streak — 248 minutes and 32 seconds — was ended. It remains an NHL playoff record.

While Smith's regular season play was just average (81–83–35), he sparkled under the pressure of playoff competition. In nine games he chalked up three shutouts and registered a 1.23 goals-against average.

Rookie Swede Stops Habs' Amazing Streak

IT WAS FEBRUARY 23, 1978, and the New York Rangers faced almost certain defeat as they prepared for a game at the Montreal Forum.

123

After all, they were mired in last place in their division and they hadn't won a game at the Forum in six years. As for the hometown Habs . . . well, the Canadiens were too hot for anyone to handle. They hadn't lost in 28 games, winning 23 and tying five. It was an NHL record, surpassing a 23-game undefeated mark shared by the 1940–41 Boston Bruins and the 1976 Philadelphia Flyers.

"We are determined to keep the streak going," Guy Lafleur told reporters. "We don't want any other team to break our record." (In time another team would — the Philadelphia Flyers.)

One of the attractions of hockey is that upsets can occur at any time. Perhaps the Rangers took to the ice that night feeling they had nothing to lose. Coach Jean-Guy Talbot must have felt that way. Otherwise why would he have plucked a nervous Swedish goaltender from the American League to face the mighty Canadiens?

Fans were stunned when 26-year-old Hardy Astrom, who would later play for Don Cherry in Colorado and be called "my Swedish sieve" among other things, was announced as the Rangers' starting goalie. Astrom had never played in an NHL game. When asked about his startling choice of goaltenders, Talbot shrugged and said, "Listen, when you play a hot team like Montreal, a coach will try anything."

It was hardly a vote of confidence, but the rookie Swede played like an All-Star. His mates, bolstered by his solid performance, checked with unfamiliar gusto, and New York skated off with a 6–3 victory. Hockey's longest undefeated streak was over — snapped by the team least likely to break it.

It was a spectacular debut for Astrom, but his

124

finest 60 minutes of NHL play were never to be duplicated. He played another 82 games in the NHL, with the Rangers and the Rockies, and compiled a dismal 17–44–12 mark.

They Didn't Stay Around Very Long

WHEN THE NHL WAS FORMED in November 1917, there were five charter members. One of the five, the Quebec Bulldogs, decided to wait another season before joining the new circuit. That left the Montreal Canadiens, the Montreal Wanderers, the Ottawa Senators, and the Toronto Arenas.

The Wanderers not only hold the record for the shortest stay in the NHL, they recorded the fewest wins. Their season was only two weeks old when, on January 2, 1918, their arena burned to the ground. Homeless, the team ceased operations and never returned. The Wanderers' proudest moment came on December 19, 1917, when they edged Toronto 10–9 in their home opener before 700 fans. It was their one and only victory in the NHL.

The Wildest Stanley Cup Parade Ever

THE HEADLINES in the Philadelphia newspapers said it all: "Miracle Flyers Take the Cup. City Goes Wild with Joy." The date was Sunday, May 19, 1974. Our NBC telecast team (Tim Ryan, Ted Lindsay, and myself) had witnessed the incredible postgame explosion of noise the day before when we covered the Flyers' thrilling Cup victory over Boston on national television.

But the celebration in the arena that Saturday afternoon was just a squeak to the pandemonium that greeted the victors the following day. Over two million Philadelphians jammed Broad Street to honor their heroes with a ticker tape parade. It was a parade that far surpassed any other Cup-winning parade in history. The streets were so crowded that several of the Flyers had to abandon their cars and push their way through the mob just to reach the mall where the open convertibles awaited them.

The crowds were so thick that the parade proceeded at a turtle's pace. The players, most of whom had been imbibing liberally since the game had ended the previous afternoon, often had to make "pit stops" to relieve themselves. They simply hopped out of their convertibles, knocked on the nearest door, and were greeted like soldiers home from a war. "Of course, you can use our facilities" was the response to every request. "All we ask in return is an autograph."

Bernie Parent and captain Bobby Clarke came in for the loudest ovations. Parent had provided coach Fred Shero's team with miraculous goaltending, and the netminder had earned the Conn Smythe Trophy as playoff MVP. Clarke's inspirational leadership was also a major reason the Flyers were able to become the first expansion team to capture Lord Stanley's old basin.

And while she declined an invitation to be part of the parade, singer Kate Smith was lauded for her role in the Flyer victory. In two playoff games Kate appeared "live" at the Spectrum to sing "God Bless

America." On both occasions the opposing team failed to score a single goal. And Kate's record as a Flyer good luck charm was simply awesome. Whenever her famous song was heard prior to a home game, the Flyers were almost unbeatable. By the end of the 1974 playoffs her mark was 37–3–1.

Home of the Face-off

THE LITTLE TOWN OF PARIS, ONTARIO, is credited with being the birthplace of hockey's face-off, while referee Fred Waghorne is recorded as its inventor. Waghorne, born in England in 1866, was a highly respected hockey referee in Canada for more than 50 years.

The distinguished official was handling a particularly difficult game in Paris one night in the early 1900s. Throughout the contest the fans supporting the teams involved screamed for their centermen to beat rival pivots to the puck. In those days, when face-offs were required, it was customary for the referee to place the puck between the sticks of the centermen, shout "Play," and jump quickly out of the way.

During the game, the opposing centermen were so eager to win the draw that Waghorne's hands, arms, and legs took a frightful beating. By the halfway mark he was bruised and bloody and he had had enough.

He told the centers before the next face-off, "You boys put your sticks on the ice and keep them 18 inches apart. And be ready for what happens next." He stood back and threw the puck between the poised sticks — like a man throwing a dog a bone.

127

Instinctively the two players clashed their sticks together in an effort to control the puck, and the modern-day face-off was born.

Waghorne was so pleased with the results of his face-off invention that he proceeded to add another innovation to refereeing. He threw away the large handbell he'd been using to signal stoppages in play and introduced a whistle. Soon all hockey officials followed suit and began using whistles, but some of them had lingering regrets over the phasing out of the handbells.

"They were very effective for keeping obnoxious fans at bay," Waghorne said. "If a fan reached out from rinkside and grabbed a player or a referee, you could wallop him over the head with the bell. He'd see stars and hear bells ringing — all at the same time."

The Cinderella Leafs Oust the Gentlemanly Rangers

IN 1958 GEORGE "PUNCH" IMLACH took over as general manager and coach of the Toronto Maple Leafs. The Leafs were mired in last place in the six-team NHL, but in the next few weeks, with Imlach cracking the whip, they caught fire. On the last night of the season the Leafs scored a come-from-behind victory over Detroit in a game the Leafs had to win to make the playoffs. Their last-night triumph, combined with a Ranger loss, put Toronto in the playoffs by a single point. The dramatic finish was front-page news across Canada, and the Leafs became hockey's latest Cinderella team.

Left in the lurch were the disappointed Rangers, coached by Phil Watson. Sometime later Watson revealed an interesting postscript to the story of that playoff race.

With the 1957–58 season winding down, Watson's Rangers were beaten one night by Boston. After the contest, Watson checked the rules and discovered that Boston had used an ineligible player in the game — a goaltender. The goalie was listed as an "emergency replacement" for the Bruins. But the regular Bruins goaltender had returned to health and there was no emergency. Watson decided to protest the game.

His boss in New York, General John Reed Kilpatrick, wouldn't hear of it. "There'll be no protest, Phil," he said. "We don't operate like that. We're gentlemen in this league."

Watson wanted to scream. Gentlemen? In hockey?

"I was certain my protest would have been upheld," he told reporters. "And the Rangers would have been awarded two more points. We would have finished one point ahead of Toronto and been in the playoffs. But it never happened because, well, I guess it's because we're gentlemen."

Richard Suspension Leads to Hockey's Biggest Riot

LATE IN THE 1954–55 SEASON the Montreal Canadiens were playing the Boston Bruins at the Boston Garden. With the Bruins leading by two goals, Montreal coach Dick Irvin pulled goalie Jacques Plante and threw an extra attacker onto the ice. Rocket Richard, the Habs' ace scorer, was racing over the Bruin blue line when Boston defenseman Hal Laycoe clipped him across the head with his stick. Referee Frank Udvari signaled a delayed penalty, and when the official blew his whistle, Richard sought immediate vengeance. He rushed over to Laycoe, raised his stick, and lashed out at him.

Linesman Cliff Thompson grabbed Richard and wrestled his stick away. But Richard broke free, picked up a loose stick lying on the ice, and attacked Laycoe a second time. He was held momentarily by Thompson, then broke loose again, grabbed yet another stick, and went right back after the Boston player. In the melee Richard punched linesman Thompson, giving him a black eye, and moments later he threw a blood-soaked towel at referee Udvari. Richard was thrown out of the game and fined $100. Any further punishment would be doled out by NHL president Clarence Campbell.

On March 16 Campbell stunned Richard by suspending him for the rest of the season and for all playoff games. Richard was outraged and so were his countless loyal fans. Callers phoned the NHL offices in Montreal, and many were so furious that they threatened Campbell's life.

The following night, March 17, the Canadiens hosted the Detroit Red Wings at the Forum. Campbell stubbornly insisted on occupying his regular place in the stands, accompanied by his secretary (and future wife) Phyllis King.

Perhaps if Montreal, battling Detroit for first

130

The man who touched off a riot: the Canadiens' Rocket Richard in full throttle.

place, had grabbed an early lead over the Red Wings, the crowd would have settled down and ignored Campbell. But Montreal fell behind 4–2, and with each Red Wing goal Campbell and Miss King were subjected to much verbal abuse. Then programs, paper cups, and other garbage were thrown at them. Suddenly a tear gas bomb went off and people panicked. They scrambled over seats and into the aisles, seeking the nearest exits. Police moved in and their quick action probably averted a major disaster. The game was stopped and later forfeited to Detroit. Campbell and Miss King were escorted to a nearby dressing room where they were temporarily safe.

131

Outside the Forum the mood of the fans, ugly to begin with, turned vicious. A mob spirit was unleashed that led to vandalism and violence. Cars were damaged, store windows were broken, and shops were looted.

Campbell would say later, "I'm convinced the riot that night marked the initial indication of the resurgence of French nationalism in Quebec. The majority of those involved were not even hockey fans but thugs who seized the Richard incident to vent their unrest against the Anglos of which I was polarized as leader."

Jack Adams, outspoken manager of Detroit, said, "It's the reporters who've turned Richard into an idol, a player whose suspension can transform hockey fans into shrieking idiots. Well, Richard is no hero. He let his team down, he let hockey down, he let the public down."

Richard, who had slipped into the game that night almost unnoticed, felt deep regret over the incident. "I wanted to go in the streets and use a loudspeaker to tell the fans to stop their nonsense. But it wouldn't have done any good. They would have paraded me around on their shoulders."

Aside from the suspension, Richard suffered the loss of a long-sought prize — the 1955 NHL scoring crown. While he sat out the final three games of the season, teammate Boom Boom Geoffrion slipped ahead of him in the scoring race and captured the Art Ross Trophy by a single point, 75–74. Richard fans, perhaps sensing that the Rocket would never again come close to a scoring title, booed Geoffrion unmercifully when he swept the crown from the head of their hero.

She Played Like a Man

WOMEN'S HOCKEY IN CANADA goes back a hundred years. When Lord Stanley donated the Stanley Cup in 1893, girls in long skirts were already pushing pucks around the ice at the Rideau Hall rink in Ottawa. One of the best of the lady players was a lass with the intriguing name of Lulu Lemoine.

From 1915 to 1917 Cornwall, Ontario, produced a crack ladies team named the Vics. Whenever the Vics traveled to Ottawa or Montreal for games, huge crowds turned out to watch the action. Fans were particularly fascinated by the sparkling play of a girl named Albertine Lapansee, a high-scoring forward on that Cornwall team. Lapansee scored about 80 percent of her team's goals. She was slight but fast, a beautiful skater, and a remarkable stickhandler and shooter.

By 1918 Lapansee's name disappeared from the Cornwall sports pages, and as a hockey historian and researcher, I wondered why. So I journeyed to Cornwall in the summer of 1992 and met with one of Albertine's relatives, a 72-year-old man named Connie Lapansee.

"Connie," I said, "your famous aunt was the best female hockey player in Canada years ago, but in my research I can find no trace of her after 1917. Whatever happened to Albertine?"

"Brian," he replied, "she had a strange life. Albertine quit playing women's hockey after the 1917 season and moved to New York. There she had a sex change operation and became a man. Of course, she changed her name, too. When she came back

133

home sometime later, well, I should say when *he* came back home, he was known as Albert Smith. He was married by then and he and his bride opened a service station not far from Cornwall."

And that is the bizarre ending to the story of Albertine Lapansee who, for a couple of incredible seasons, was known as the best female hockey player in Canada.

PART

MARVELOUS MADCAPS

Journalist in Goal

IN THE FALL OF 1977 George Plimpton, a noted American journalist and sports fan, asked the Boston Bruins if he could play goal for them in a big league hockey game. He had never played goal before, but he wondered what an NHL goalie's life was like. He wanted to write about it. What better way to find out than to stand in the net, wearing the goaltender's armor, and face sizzling slapshots?

Bruins coach Don Cherry vetoed any notion of Plimpton playing in a regular season game but consented to let him represent the Bruins in a brief five-minute trial during a preseason game. Plimpton was also required to sign a "no-fault" contract, releasing the Bruins and the NHL from any responsibility for injuries he might suffer, including death.

Plimpton attended the Bruins' fall training camp and roomed with minor league goalie Jim Pettie, who instructed him in the fundamentals of netminding.

Cherry didn't make it easy for the literary volunteer. He decided to start Plimpton in a game against the Philadelphia Flyers at the Spectrum. In the dressing room prior to the game Gerry Cheevers, Boston's number one goalie, approached Plimpton with some last-minute advice. "Stand up! Stand up!" he said, meaning to remind him to stay upright on the ice. Plimpton misunderstood and thought Cheevers was commanding him to stand up in the dressing room. So he shot to his feet. While the other players laughed Cheevers said, "Not in here, George. Out on the ice." He turned to his mates and muttered, "What a basket case this guy is."

When the game began, Plimpton had no problems

137

for the first two minutes, for the Bruins went on the attack and kept the puck in the Flyer zone. Then the tide turned and a wave of Flyers surged into the Boston zone, and Plimpton had only a fleeting glimpse of "that awful black puck, sailing elusively between sticks and skates, as shifty as a rat in a hedgerow."

The first shot the Flyers took went in, a zinger from the point tipped in by Orest Kindrachuk. Plimpton yelled loudly in dismay and beat the side of his helmet with his blocking pad as Flyer fans, showing no sympathy, laughed at his plight.

Then Boston's Bobby Schmautz took a penalty, and Plimpton found himself facing the Flyer power play. One shot ricocheted off the crossbar. Another just missed the far corner as Plimpton sprawled awkwardly onto the ice. In an effort to get back onto his feet he grabbed a defenseman around the leg and hauled himself upright, using his surprised teammate the way a drunk might use a lamppost.

Six Flyer shots were drilled in his direction and, amazingly, none went in. One bounced off his mask. The rest hit various parts of his body. At one point during the barrage he turned completely away from the play to peer into his net, thinking a puck had eluded him. A photographer jumped up and snapped a shot of him, staring into the depths of the goal, like a man looking for an escape route, while the action raged furiously in front of his crease.

Later, writing about his NHL debut in *Sports Illustrated,* Plimpton would take no credit for any of the saves. He was, he said, "somewhat akin to a tree in the line of flight of a golf ball."

138

With the author's five-minute stint just about over, Boston's Mike Milbury threw a stick at an incoming Flyer forward and a penalty shot was called. Reg Leach, who had once scored 61 goals in a season, was the shooter. Leach raced in from center ice. Plimpton moved out to cut down the shooting angle and collapsed like a house of cards just as Leach fired. Eyes closed, Plimpton felt the shot graze his goal skate and deflect high into the crowd.

The Bruins surged off the bench and hauled George upright. They cuffed him with their gloves and dragged him over to the bench. "They handled me like a sack of potatoes," he later wrote. "Of course, they told me Leach was a psychological ruin after he failed to beat me. And they said I'd made 30 or 40 saves at least in my brief appearance."

After his ordeal on the ice, Plimpton knew he "belonged as a Bruin" when he began to get dressed. His tie was chopped in half, the toes had been snipped from his socks, and the seat was gone from his underwear.

Cherry said to him, "George, you should feel honored. And lucky, too. When my guys initiate someone, usually the hair goes, too."

Last Link to Ballard's Leafs

FEW NHL ORGANIZATIONS have had mascots as famous as T. C. Puck, the shaggy dog that supported some dreadful Leaf teams during the eighties. T. C. Puck was a gift from 58-year-old Yolanda (MacMillan) Ballard to her friend

139

and lover, octogenarian Harold Ballard, several months prior to his death on April 11, 1990.

Puck, a Bouvier des Flandres, appeared in Leaf team photos and made the Gardens his personal dog kennel. He was once the center of a dispute between Yolanda and a Gardens employee who was ordered to walk the mascot. When the employee refused, Yolanda persuaded Ballard to have the employee fired.

After Ballard's death, Yolanda went to court, seeking a $12,000-a-month living allowance for the dog so he could continue to live in the Ballard lifestyle. But the Bouvier, like Ballard, was living on borrowed time. His demise took place suddenly two days before Christmas 1991. The dog suffered a massive heart attack in the back seat of a cab while returning from his favorite animal clinic, where he had been groomed and given a clip-and-curl with "not too much off the sides, if you please."

According to the cabbie, Yolanda "panicked" when Puck collapsed. Then, to the driver's astonishment, she began to give Puck mouth-to-mouth resuscitation in a valiant attempt to revive him.

"She was in a state of shock," he said. "She was crying. To her it was like losing a child."

Puck was rushed back to the clinic where attendants carried him inside on a stretcher. Ballard insisted on an autopsy, and when veterinarians said they couldn't perform one, she had the dog loaded back into the cab.

When they arrived at Ballard's house, the cabbie was recruited to help drag the dog inside. Puck was placed in a cool spot until Yolanda could arrange for an autopsy. Later in the day she and her daugh-

140

ter Anna drove Puck to the University of Guelph's veterinary hospital where they were told nothing could be done. Later a tearful Yolanda told reporters she would arrange for "a proper burial and a tombstone" for her famous pet.

The story of T. C. Puck's demise was in all the papers. He was one of the last links to Ballard's Leafs.

Hockey's Biggest Practical Joker

WHEN FUN-LOVING NICK FOTIU retired from hockey, his teammates breathed a sigh of relief. No longer would they have to be on guard against the game's biggest practical joker.

Many of Fotiu's most notorious pranks took place when he played for the New York Rangers. He learned, for example, that teammate Phil Esposito abhorred bugs, especially cockroaches. So Fotiu delighted in swatting roaches — just enough to stun them — and depositing the ugly little insects in with Espo's hockey equipment. When Espo reached for a jock strap or an elbow pad, he was apt to be greeted by a creepy-crawly that would drive him berserk. On another occasion, when Esposito carelessly left a brand-new pair of white golf shoes in the Ranger dressing room, Fotiu painted them bright orange.

Fotiu was known to substitute shaving cream for whipped cream on the dessert tray in restaurants, to put talcum powder in the dressing room hair

141

dryers, and to swab black shoe polish on the ear-piece of telephone receivers. Once he placed a live lobster on the chest of his sleeping roommate Bill Goldsworthy, whose screams on awakening could be heard for miles. Another time Fotiu hid in a hotel room closet and waited there until his roommate woke up and started to get dressed. When the roomie reached in the closet for his shirt and jacket, Fotiu grabbed him around the throat, scaring the tar out of him.

If Fotiu happened to rise in the morning before his roommate, he would turn on the shower, close the bathroom door, and go down for breakfast. The unsuspecting roommate would eventually get up, hear the shower sounds, and wait patiently for his turn under the spray — and wait and wait and wait.

From time to time teammates exacted revenge on the impish Fotiu. Goalie John Davidson, often a victim of Fotiu's elaborate pranks, recalls the time he pilfered Fotiu's truck keys out of a pocket, started the vehicle, and turned on the lights, the heater, the radio, the windshield wipers — everything. Then he left the keys inside and locked the doors.

One night Davidson led a Ranger attack force to Fotiu's house where they toilet-papered everything in sight. Trees, the family car, the house itself — everything was covered in toilet paper. Then Davidson called the police, told them a man was trapped in a house, and gave them Fotiu's address. When the police arrived and pounded on Fotiu's door, the astonished hockey player was at a loss to explain his papered property.

Davidson recalls how upset he was the day he caught Fotiu red-handed in the middle of a practical joke. He happened to look out a restaurant window to see Fotiu filling Davidson's car with garbage from cans on the street corner.

The goalie also recalls the time Fotiu discovered that most of the Rangers had traveling bags with little keys attached — keys that were seldom if ever used. When the trainers piled the luggage onto the team bus one day, Fotiu unobtrusively locked all the bags and pocketed the keys. When the players checked into their hotel rooms and tried to open their bags, there was enough cursing and shouting to bring a hotel detective running.

Fotiu might have come running, too, for angry epithets were always music to his ears. But he was too busy laughing.

The Goalie Was a Golfer

IN THE EARLY SEVENTIES goalie Ed Johnston of the Boston Bruins was seeking a raise. He told Boston executive vice president Charles Mulcahy he wanted a modest increase, enough to bring his salary to $20,000 a year. Mulcahy, in reply, said he didn't think Johnston's work in goal merited that amount. When the two men failed to reach an agreement, Mulcahy, who was a scratch golfer, challenged Johnston to a golf match — three holes at Mulcahy's course. If Johnston won, he would get his raise. The odds appeared to favor Mulcahy because he had won several golf tournaments and had even

143

represented the U.S. internationally at one point in his career.

But Johnston was a capable golfer, too, and had lots of experience wrestling with par. "Let's make the stakes double or nothing," he suggested. "If I win, you pay me $40,000 a year. If I lose, there'll be no raise."

Mulcahy laughed. "You're on. See you on the tee."

On the day of the match Johnston's drives were long and straight, his putting superb, and he beat his boss over the three holes they played. Only after he signed the check that doubled Johnston's salary did Mulcahy learn that his goaltender had already established himself as one of the finest golfers ever to play professional hockey.

Johnston went on to become a successful general manager in the NHL, first with Pittsburgh, then with Hartford. In Pittsburgh he signed Mario Lemieux to

Goalie Ed Johnston when he played for the Toronto Maple Leafs.

144

one of the richest contracts in hockey history. But Johnston never once suggested a golf match to determine Mario's salary. For Lemieux's golfing prowess is awesome, and he would be more than a match for any general manager.

Miro the Zero

WHEN GERRY MCNAMARA was general manager of the Leafs (1982–1988), he acquired two Czech players, Peter Ihnacak and Miroslav Frycer, and he wanted more. When he heard that Ihnacak had a younger brother Miro, who was reputed to be a scoring star back home, he got goose bumps.

Miro Ihnacak had never been scouted by the Leafs. No one in the Leaf organization even knew what he looked like. The Leafs, through a negotiator, arranged for Ihnacak's defection from Czechoslovakia. The immigration process that helped speed the young star's arrival in Canada was spurred by federal sports minister Otto Jelinek, a native of Czechoslovakia. It was rumored that young Miro was an awesome physical specimen — six foot two and close to 200 pounds.

When he finally stepped onto the ice at Maple Leaf Gardens to display his skills, onlookers were shocked. He was a lightweight and no taller than five-nine. And his skating, stickhandling, and shooting were average.

It didn't take the media long to get on his case. His nickname became Miro the Zero, and in 56 games as a Leaf he scored a mere eight goals. He proved to be one of the most expensive flops in

145

hockey history, costing the Toronto club close to a million dollars in fees, salary, and expenses to spirit him out of his native land and give him an all-too-brief taste of life in the NHL.

Have Résumé, Will Travel

WHEN THE NHL DOUBLED its six teams in 1967, dozens of players were drafted by the new franchises. Young kids who were as green as grass and old pros who had toiled in the minors for years found themselves on big league rosters. Nobody was overlooked.

One was. For 17 years hard-rock defenseman Larry Zeidel had bulled his way through three minor leagues, leading all of them in penalty minutes. If any of the expansion teams considered him at all, their assessment was "too old" or "washed up." But Zeidel had absolute confidence in his ability and soon found a novel way to sell himself to the new owners.

He invested $150 and prepared a glossy résumé, extolling his virtues as a player and as a hockey executive. "Why not?" Zeidel asked. "That's the way you get a good job in the business world." The résumés were mailed to all six expansion teams, and most of them, predictably, found their way into the nearest wastebasket. But Keith Allen, general manager of the Philadelphia Flyers, read one through and was impressed. He contacted Zeidel and offered him a tryout.

"There's just one snag," Zeidel said. "I still belong to Cleveland of the American League. But let me deal with that."

146

The resourceful player quickly arranged a conference call with the Cleveland owner and talked the deal into completion. To that point in his career, Zeidel had spent nearly 2,500 minutes in the penalty box, time equal to more than 40 full games.

Even though he had been away from the NHL since 1954, Zeidel had no difficulty making the Flyers' roster and helping them to a first-place finish in the West Division of the NHL. After a second season with the team, he retired from the game.

When Weldy Lost His Temper

BACK IN 1898 WELDY YOUNG was a hot-tempered player with the Ottawa hockey club. During a playoff game that year, Weldy was having an off night and the fans started to jeer his play. Young ignored the razzing for a while, but when one loudmouth in the crowd got under his skin, he decided it was time to do something. Spotting the critic, Weldy leaped over the boards and went after him. The fans in the area scattered, for Young's mean streak was renowned, and it looked as if the fan he had targeted was in for a beating. But the fan had several friends in the crowd, and Young soon discovered he had bitten off more than he could chew. The spectators ganged up on him and pummeled him into submission. Somehow, bruised and bloody, the Ottawa tough guy was able to stagger back onto the ice and resume play.

Weldy Young wasn't a well-liked player, even by his own teammates. When the team manager decided to make room for Young on the Ottawa roster

147

one season, the club president resigned and two players, Chauncey Kirby and goaltender Fred Chittick, said they would play no more.

Not Your Normal Pregame Meal

THE LATE GEORGE HAYES, one of hockey's most colorful and eccentric linesmen, liked to save a little money on road trips by packing his own lunches. One day he packed some canned meat and fresh bread in his bag, added a "bottle or two" to wash things down, and jumped onto the train for Detroit.

En route, spurning the costly dining car, he opened the canned meat, spread the contents onto the bread, added thick chunks of onion on top, and sat back to enjoy his meal. It was only when he went to throw the empty can into the trash that he noticed a photo of a dog on the label.

"I admit I had a snort or two beforehand," he told his pal, referee Red Storey, when they met before the game in Detroit. "But I can't believe I made sandwiches out of dog food. Whatever you do, Red, don't breathe a word of this to anybody."

Red assured him he wouldn't, but Red was never one to keep quiet, not when a good laugh was assured. When the players took to the ice for their pregame warm-up, some of them skated close to Hayes.

"Arf, Arf!" they barked. "Ruff, ruff."

"They kept barkin' at me all game," Hayes said. Some of them even called me 'Pard.' I was ready to kill that big mouth Storey."

148

Pass the Damn Puck, Regan!

WHEN I WAS A KID playing endless games of shinny on an Ottawa playground rink, whenever Larry Regan showed up to play, the rest of us groaned. He was too good for most of us, an extremely talented stickhandler and scorer. Maybe that was why he seldom passed the puck. If you played on Larry's side in our pickup games, you seldom got any passes.

After playing Junior A hockey with the Toronto Marlboros and kicking around the minors for a few seasons, Regan joined the Boston Bruins at the ripe old age of 26 and won the Calder Trophy as rookie of the year. Regan enjoyed five NHL seasons with two clubs — Boston and Toronto — and in 1968 he turned up as a coach and general manager of the Los Angeles Kings of the expanded NHL. By the time he reached the NHL he had rid himself of his puck-hogging habits.

Perhaps it was in Pembroke, Ontario (one of his minor league stops), that he learned a lesson about making better use of his linemates. One night Regan was stickhandling all over the ice and completely ignoring his wingers. One of his mates, Rheal Savard, kept rapping his stick on the ice in frustration, calling for a pass. When Regan finally spotted Savard in the clear and whipped the puck in his direction, the winger had grown weary of waiting. He snared the pass, flipped the puck from his stick to his glove, and skated over to his team's bench. He handed the disk to trainer Bill Higginson and said, "Here, Bill, get this damn thing mounted. It's the first bloody pass I've got from Regan all season."

149

Chatty Pat Riggin Talks Himself into a Trade

IN THE SPRING OF 1985 Canada's team at the World Hockey Championships in Prague, Czechoslovakia, needed help. The NHL, as was customary, sent over several players to bolster Team Canada — players plucked from teams that had been eliminated from the playoffs. Even though Canada had experienced only marginal success using this approach in the past, this time the NHL players parachuted in were a big help. One of the stars in the tournament was goalie Pat Riggin of the Washington Capitals.

The Canadians just missed winning a gold medal when they suffered a final-game loss to the Czechs. After the tournament, Riggin told reporters about his delight in whipping the U.S. team because he didn't particularly like the Americans. He said he didn't like the ones who were taking NHL jobs away from Canadian boys.

Perhaps he thought his remarks would never be reported outside of Czechoslovakia. If so, he was wrong. Almost overnight his comments were splashed across the sports pages of dozens of papers in Canada and the United States. Naturally his anti-American stance outraged Washington Capital fans, not to mention some of Riggin's teammates on the Caps, a few of whom happened to be American-born.

Riggin tried to explain that his remarks were directed merely at the players on the U.S. team in Prague. "They were cocky and arrogant and we were out to beat them. I was trying for an edge," he said.

150

But most Cap fans didn't buy his explanation. They called the hockey club office and wrote letters, registering their displeasure and even rage. Not surprisingly, the Caps dumped their talkative goaltender a few months later, trading him to the Boston Bruins.

But, Coach, I Was Watching the Replay

FORMER NHL GOALTENDER John Garrett, now a *Hockey Night in Canada* broadcaster, will never forget the most embarrassing moment in his career. He was the starting goalie for the Hartford Whalers one night in Washington. One of the things that fascinated Garrett about the Washington arena was the huge screen on the scoreboard over center ice, a screen that enabled fans to watch video replays of goals and other exciting plays.

Broadcaster John Garrett in his goaltending days.

151

Garrett was pleased with his performance that night, and by the midway point of the hockey game he had robbed the Caps of several goal-scoring opportunities. But suddenly he had to deal with a two-on-one situation. Two Cap players skated into the Hartford zone. The lone Whaler defenseman fell down while trying to intercept a pass, and one of the Caps slipped the puck through Garrett's pads into the net.

Recalling the incident, Garrett says, "I couldn't believe they'd beaten me on the play. I was sure the puck didn't quite cross the goal line. So I looked up at the big screen to watch the replay. Perhaps it would confirm I was right.

"While I was watching the replay the referee dropped the puck and play resumed. The Washington centerman won the draw and slipped the puck over to hard-shooting Mike Gartner. He stepped over the blue line and rifled a shot in my direction. But I didn't see the puck coming because I was still watching the replay on the giant screen.

"That's when I heard my teammates screaming at me to wake up, and suddenly I knew I'd made a terrible faux pas. I tried to recover and focus on the slapshot headed straight for my net, but it was too late. The puck zipped past me and the Caps scored a second goal — all in a matter of seconds. It was almost a record for the two fastest goals.

"Coach Don Blackburn waved me over to the bench and told me to sit down. 'You can watch the next replay from the end of the bench,' he snapped as he made a goaltending change. My face was so red I wouldn't even take my goal mask off."

152

A Strange Penalty Shot Call

LOTS OF NHL PLAYERS get to take a penalty shot in their careers, and two players, Pat Egan and Greg Terrion, even share a record of scoring two penalty shot goals in a season. In the seventies Phil Hoene, a Los Angeles Kings rookie, scored his first NHL goal on a penalty shot, while Chicago goalie Michel Belhumeur once stopped two penalty shots in one game. But only one NHL player has ever scored on two free shots within a matter of seconds.

It happened in the forties when Jackie Hamilton was a budding young star with the Toronto Maple Leafs. Hamilton was pulled down by Boston's Dit Clapper one night, and the referee awarded him a penalty shot. But in those days the league rules called for two types of penalty shots — a major and a minor. For a major penalty shot the referee spotted the puck at center ice and the player taking the shot moved in on the goalie and shot from point-blank range — just as they do today. But for a minor penalty shot the puck was spotted 28 feet out from the goal and the player — without being able to move in on goal — fired it from there.

When Hamilton was preparing for his free shot, the referee became confused. He placed the puck at center ice, not at the 28-foot mark where it belonged. Hamilton promptly grabbed the disk, raced in, and scored.

Then a loud argument erupted. The rival coach banged the boards and pointed out the referee's mistake. He maintained the shot had been taken from the wrong point. Everyone's temper rose

153

except Hamilton's. Finally the referee said, "Jackie, you're going to have to take the shot over again, this time from inside the blue line."

"Fine with me," the obliging Hamilton said. "You're the boss."

Hamilton lined up, blasted a hard shot past the goaltender, and skated away, grinning. Two penalty shots, two pucks in the net. "Yeah," Hamilton said later, laughing, "but I only got credit for one of them."

Be My Guest

HALL OF FAME GOALTENDER Bill Durnan played for the Montreal Canadiens in the forties and captured the Vezina Trophy six times in seven seasons. Long after his career was over, Durnan confessed he had one lingering regret: he hadn't had the courage to emulate a stunt perpetrated by another pro goalie — Alec Woods.

Woods toiled throughout his career in the American Hockey League and performed in only one NHL game, with the New York Americans in 1937. "Alec was born in Falkirk, Scotland," Durnan recalled, "and he had a reputation for being thrifty. That's why I was surprised at his amazing display of generosity one night. Woods's team failed to give him much support in the game I'm talking about, and goal after goal sailed into his net. Finally the score reached 8–0 and there were only a few seconds left to play.

"Suddenly Woods braced himself for yet another challenge as an opposing forward raced toward him, cradling the puck. The player looked for an opening and prepared to shoot. That's when

154

Alec did something completely unheard of, something I later wanted to try in the NHL but didn't dare. Just as the player wound up for his shot, Alec grinned at him and stepped aside. He waved his goal stick at the empty net and said, 'Be my guest.'

"The startled shooter laughed and said, 'Thanks, goalie,' as he slipped the disk into the goal. I'd never heard of such a thing happening in professional hockey. I don't think anything like it has happened since."

Krutov the Critic

DURING THE 1983–84 SEASON, Soviet hockey star Vladimir Krutov, then 23, took some potshots at Wayne Gretzky, the best player in the NHL.

"He's not very fast, but he does handle the stick perfectly," Krutov stated. "However, his physique leaves much to be desired. On the whole he's a good player, but I don't think he'd perform as well in the Soviet league as he does in the NHL."

Gretzky, who was coming off his best month ever (49 points), said little. But he must have been chuckling in 1989 when a rather bloated Krutov signed a huge contract to come to North America to play for the Vancouver Canucks.

Critics noted that the Russian star wasn't very fast and his physique left much to be desired. "He can stickhandle past everything but a McDonald's," one Canuck said after watching the overweight import struggle up the ice. As soon as he completed one mediocre season in Vancouver, Krutov took his fading

155

skills, and his impressive appetite, to a European league.

Shortest Career in History

IN THE THIRTIES the Toronto Maple Leafs, with several players sidelined with injuries, limped into the NHL playoffs one year. Desperate for help, the team called on a local lad, Shrimp McPherson, to don the blue and white. In the event of another injury Shrimp would get his big league chance.

Midway through the game Shrimp's big moment came. He was instructed to replace an injured Leaf who was hobbling toward the bench. In his excitement and eagerness to play, Shrimp jumped onto the ice too soon. His skates no sooner hit the Gardens' slick surface when the referee signaled a penalty, pointing at him.

"Too many men on the ice," he roared. Red-faced, Shrimp McPherson headed back to the bench while one of his teammates was sent to the penalty box. Thus, jumping over the boards was the extent of Shrimp's NHL career, and he has the dubious distinction of being the only player in NHL history to be the cause of a penalty, even though he failed to play a single second in the NHL.

Now It Can Be Told

THE BOSTON BRUINS WERE one of the first NHL clubs to sign a Swedish player. They had high hopes for Sven (Tumba) Johanson,

156

a four-time Olympian who joined the Bruins at training camp over 30 years ago. Johanson's stay in the NHL was a brief one, however, mainly because of a practical joke he concocted.

"I don't think the Bruins accepted me," he said on his return to Sweden, "and I think it was because of a practical joke I played on them one day. I saw that they all joked around with each other in the dressing room, and I wanted to be a part of it. So I asked myself what I could do to become accepted by them. Well, I noticed that they all put their false teeth in little cups before a game or practice. So I thought I'd have some fun. When they went onto the ice, I sneaked back in the room and switched all the teeth around. When they came back in, they found that none of their teeth fitted.

"Did they laugh at my little prank? No, were they ever mad. And they knew it was me who'd done it because I was laughing like crazy. From then on it was very cool between us, and a few days later the manager took me aside and told me he was sending me back to Sweden."

You're on the Wrong Bench, Picard

WHEN THE ST. LOUIS BLUES joined the NHL as an expansion team in 1968, one of their most popular players was a big defenseman named Noel Picard. But there were nights when Picard didn't appear to be totally focused on the game.

Midway through an important game against Boston

157

Picard finished his shift and headed for the bench. Problem was, he went to the Bruins' bench by mistake. Maybe he was thinking about how to stop Bobby Orr or Phil Esposito. Perhaps, subconsciously, he wanted to get away from the sharp tongue of his coach, Scotty Bowman. He was never able to explain his action.

The Boston trainer, Frosty Forrestal, when he saw Picard approaching, opened the gate to the bench and waved him in. Picard found a spot on the pine, sat down, and play resumed. Only when he looked around did he notice something strange — everyone around him was wearing Boston colors.

What to do? The players and fans were laughing at his predicament, while across the rink Blues coach Scotty Bowman was livid and shaking a fist in his direction. Squirming with embarrassment, Picard decided to act. When the play went into the Bruins' zone, he leaped over the boards, dashed across the ice, and dived in among his teammates. He was praying nobody would notice his three-second sprint to the home team bench.

Alas, out of the corner of his eye, the referee had spotted Picard's leap off the Bruins' bench and blew his whistle just as the red-faced defenseman scrambled over the boards on the far side of the rink.

"Too many men on the ice!" he barked as he penalized the Blues for two minutes, causing Scotty Bowman's blood pressure to soar even higher.

As for Picard, he put his head down like a whipped dog. He knew his gaffe would provide a million laughs for hockey people for decades to come.

Take Your Best Shot, Grandma!

IN WINNIPEG A FEW YEARS AGO a 48-year-old grandmother rivaled any pro player in the NHL for shooting accuracy. And in doing so she won a cool $58,000 in prize money.

Joan Palmer, a grandmother of four, was selected to try her shooting luck during the intermission of a Winnipeg Jet–Detroit Red Wing game at the Winnipeg Arena. Her challenge was to shoot a three-inch puck through a tiny three-and-a-quarter-inch opening 120 feet away.

Grandma Palmer was allowed just one shot, and she turned it into the shot of a lifetime. The puck slid straight toward the net and slipped through the hole. Her prize was $58,000 — five times her annual salary as a Pink Lady Courier.

But Joan Palmer wasn't the only female Winnipeg fan involved in such a competition. On another occasion a female shooter whacked the puck from center ice into the corner of the rink, missing the net by several feet. The crowd groaned. But her puck hit another puck on the ice, left there by a previous shooter. The crowd urged officials to give the woman another chance. What could they lose? So they called her back and gave her a second shot, a rare concession. This time her shot went straight toward the goal and slid through the narrow opening, making her the proud winner of two new automobiles.

159

Wayne Gretzky Stole My Car

MIDWAY THROUGH THE THIRD PERIOD of the 1983 All-Star game on Long Island, the Campbell Conference All-Stars held a 5–2 lead over their Wales Conference rivals. It was an exciting moment for Campbell Conference goalie John Garrett, then with the Vancouver Canucks. Garrett was an emergency replacement for the Canucks' number one netminder Richard Brodeur, who was sidelined with an injury.

"I was probably the only player ever to appear in an All-Star game without ever acquiring any votes to help get me there," Garrett said later. "Anyway, as the game progressed shots kept hitting me and I made some good saves and Lanny McDonald kept reminding me I was in line to win a new car as the game's MVP. Hey, wouldn't that be a thrill?

"After I made a particularly good save, Lanny skated over to me and said, 'Great stop, John. That gets you the tires and the license plate.' After another save he said, 'Now you've got the engine and the frame.' And after a third save he said, 'They'll have to give you the keys to it now, John.'

"The car was a new Camaro Z-28, and I was beginning to think it would look very pretty sitting in my garage. I was told later that the sportswriters who did the voting were leaning heavily in my direction. Midway through the final period the name Garrett was on all of their ballots.

"Then, just as the ballots were about to be collected, Wayne Gretzky scored a goal for the Campbells. Lanny skated right over to me and said, 'I don't know, John. There goes the trunk.' A few minutes later Gretzky scored again and Lanny said,

160

'There goes the steering wheel, John.' When Gretzky popped in a third goal, Lanny shrugged and said, 'I think Wayne just found the keys, Johnny.' And when Gretzky scored a record fourth goal in the period, Lanny shook his head and said, 'John, I think he just stole the damn car right out of your driveway.'

"Meanwhile, up in the press box, the writers were busy erasing my name from their ballots and writing in Gretzky's." Garrett smiled. "Aw, but he deserved to win it, even if it was the 13th car he'd won in hockey."

A Hockey Stick for the Prime Minister

TEAM CANADA HAD JUST DEFEATED the Soviets in the memorable 1972 hockey "series of the century," and all Canadians rejoiced. In Moscow, Team Canada assistant coach John Ferguson, thinking ahead perhaps to the days when he would be telling his grandchildren all about the stunning victory, was busy collecting autographs. He brought a hockey stick to the Soviet dressing room and had the players sign it: Tretiak, Kharlamov, Petrov, and all the rest.

The Canadian players signed Fergie's stick, too: Clarke, Dryden, Savard and, of course, Paul Henderson. The stick, cluttered with signatures, was a memento he would treasure forever.

When Team Canada arrived back home, a huge reception awaited them at Dorval Airport in Montreal. As the players disembarked, they passed through a reception line where they were greeted

Tough guy John Ferguson bags a goal for the Montreal Canadiens.

and congratulated by Prime Minister Pierre Elliott Trudeau.

Ferguson, clutching his souvenir stick, was preceded in the line by his close friend and former Montreal teammate Serge Savard. Savard and the prime minister exchanged pleasantries and then, to Fergie's consternation, he heard Savard say, "Mr. Prime Minister, look what John Ferguson has brought you all the way from Moscow. A souvenir hockey stick autographed by all the players."

"Thank you, John," Trudeau said, reaching for the stick. "How thoughtful of you. What a nice surprise."

What could Fergie do? He handed over the stick. At the same time it was all he could do to refrain from throttling Savard on the spot.

A few days later a reporter heard about Savard's

162

practical joke and printed the story of the souvenir stick. The prime minister read the article and called Fergie. "John, I'm perfectly willing to send the stick back to you."

"Naw, that's okay," Fergie replied. "You're welcome to it."

On the golf course with Fergie last summer I asked him about that long-ago incident. "Fergie, I can't believe he really kept the stick, even though you told him to. He must have known how much it meant to you. Why didn't he just return it?"

Fergie sighed. "I dunno. All I know is he kept it."